Praise for Faith

Eddie Tokpa's thoughtful and heartfelt memoir is an invitation. It is an invitation to accompany a boy in his daily struggle growing up a son of an impoverished rubber tapper on a Firestone plantation in Liberia; an invitation to run with him as he flees in terror from the brutality of civil war; an invitation to see with his eyes and feel with his body the pangs of hunger, the despair of homelessness, and the anxiety of a future seemingly without hope. It is an invitation to accompany Eddie as he engages with nameless and faceless bureaucrats who, with no thought to the strokes of their pens determine the course and direction of his life. It is an invitation to hold his hand as he faces a diagnosis of a life-threatening cancer.

But Eddie's invitation to us is also to be a part of his journey of faith, as he discovers and comes to love and trust a God who is present with him in every circumstance. It is an invitation to learn of women and men who, in their own lives of faith become Jesus' hands and feet, offering Eddie support, companionship, and healing. It is about faith, love, and hope in the face of devastating circumstances that are usually for most of us only headlines, statistics, and ignorance. So, why read this book? Because in a world where we can and do so easily change the news channel and ignore the pain of a desperately hurting world, Eddie offers us the opportunity to witness redemption and hope. And perhaps enable us to see and act as disciples of Jesus are called.

Dr. Paul Robinson
Professor Emeritus, Wheaton College (IL)
Co-founder, Congo Initiative & The Christian Bilingual University of Congo (UCBC)

As an international worker with thirty years of experience working with marginalized people including refugees in global settings, I found this book extremely helpful to understand the plight of refugees and how to help.

Linda Watt
SIM missionary

In a haunting and harrowing journey, Eddie's courage, resilience, and strength is a gift to us—to reframe suffering and pain, and to find the hope that we all long for. The narrative arc is ultimately an exploration of what it means to find *home*, literally and figuratively amidst great seasons of disruption, upheaval, disorientation, and waiting. And the answer, though nuanced throughout the book, is also stated simply as found in the One who carried him through. Eddie's unquenchable spirit and the love that sees him through every hardship, turns this harrowing tale into hallowed ground.

Rev. Julie Merritt Lee
Spiritual Director

Eddie will take you on a trek through unimaginable hardships, where you will feel the horrors of this broken and fallen world. Then God pours grace into Eddie's life, and you will see divine intervention at every single step of his amazing journey.

Eddie's life is inexplicable outside of the reality and power of Jesus Christ! This aptly-titled book is sure to build up *your* faith and resilience – two virtues we sorely need, to thrive in this broken and fallen world.

Jim Walters

Retired Pastor, Bear Valley Church
Executive Director, Servantsintl.org

This memoir by Eddie Tokpa is a blessing to all who seek to understand more deeply what it is like to grow up in a situation of poverty and oppression, survive the horrors of a civil war, live in a refugee camp for years on end, struggle with the bureaucracies of the US visa system, and battle serious cancer. Along with that, though, it is also a testimony to perseverance and hope nurtured by faith in Jesus Christ in the face of abysmal odds, to the way that these can transform challenges into insights, and how God can and does use each one of us individually and corporately as the body of Christ to make a huge difference in the lives of those in need as we seek to be faithful to that calling. By the time you finish reading this book, you will most likely be asking yourself: who might God be calling me to come alongside right now?

David Bronkema

Professor and Templeton Chair for
Christian Service through Entrepreneurship
Eastern University

We hear a lot about warfare, displaced people, and refugee camps in our world today. Eddie Tokpa's autobiography is a well-written account giving an amazing opportunity to experience vicariously what it's like to live through war, displacement, and being a refugee. But this man's life story is also an epic adventure of survival, incredible resilience, and, yes, unimaginable suffering. Amid that, Eddie discovered the grit he needed to persevere through life's hard times, the resilience and unshakeable joy of Jesus, and taking advantage of every opportunity that came his way for education until he got his master's degree. Finally, Eddie reveals his battle against multiple myeloma. This is an amazing story.

David Mai

---

faith
and
resilience

faith and resilience

A Refugee's Journey to Peace

EDDIE TOKPA

MEDIA.COM

Faith and Resilience

Published by
Illumify Media Global
www.IllumifyMedia.com
"Let's bring your book to life!"

Paperback ISBN: 978-1-959099-87-1

Cover design by Debbie Lewis

Printed in the United States of America

I dedicate this book to my wife, Lisa! Life is a team sport. I can't think of anyone better to have on my team than you. Thank you for your outpouring of support, steadfast commitment and sacrificial love. Thank you for believing in my dream!

Contents

Foreword

My imagination sent me to wild places before we left for a summer in Africa. Those wild places, I learned later, were excessively romantic and highly prejudiced. Romantic because we would be living on the savannah and seeing animals in Africa roaming free that are confined to zoos in America. Romantic because I would be teaching African students in their world, not mine. Romantic because our family would embark on this adventure together. It was the ultimate family experience.

And prejudiced because I thought of Africa as a monoculture. Prejudiced because I assumed I would witness nothing but inefficiency and poverty. Prejudiced because it would not measure up to my American standards.

I was wrong on all counts. Every one of my preconceptions—both romanticized and prejudicial—were exposed and challenged. And all for one reason.

Relationships with African people.

During the summer of 2000 I traveled to Kenya to teach at Daystar University. My three children, Catherine, then 17, David, then 15, and John, then 11, traveled with me. I taught at Daystar's rural campus, which is where we also lived. My children did volunteer work at an orphanage in Nairobi while I taught. Having been recently widowed, I led my three children into the unknown with a great deal of ambivalence, not aware of the surprises that awaited us.

The experience exceeded all expectations.

Eddie Tokpa is one reason why. My son, a competitive runner, began to run with Eddie in the savannah. Eddie soon became a family friend. He has remained our friend over the years. I am honored that he would ask me to write the Forward for this wonderful book.

Eddie began to think about writing a memoir a number of years ago. He sent me a sample chapter for my evaluation. The chapter told the story of his harrowing escape from Liberia after civil war erupted. I sent him some comments and encouraged him to continue with the project.

Little did I know what he would do with it. What you are about to read is a powerful piece of writing. It is also hard to classify. It is a memoir, to be sure. But it is so unusual that it defies classification. It almost requires a new word to capture its essence.

For one, it reads like a novel. He situates his own story, as dramatic as it is, in a larger narrative, which includes flight from civil war, separation from family and friends, confinement in a refugee camp, university education, love and marriage, battles with ill-health, and more. It was like reading an updated version of *Les Miserable*, with Eddie the new Jean Valjean. I learned much about his story that I didn't know. I learned even more about the collision of cultures, the thirst for power, which often leads to injustice, western prejudice and bureaucracy, and the buoyancy and courage of the human spirit.

Eddie splashes his story on a big canvas. He grows up in Liberia, finds his way to a refugee camp, studies in Kenya, falls in love in Africa but courts her at a distance, lives again in Liberia, then America, then Uganda, and finally in America. It is a dramatic tale, almost fictional. Except that it is not. I know Eddie. I have followed his movements for years. It is all the more amazing to me that his story is true.

Eddie also demonstrates an unusual capacity for reflection. Throughout the book he muses on what it means to survive in a sometimes-unfriendly world. He learns to negotiate byzantine bureaucracies. He endures constant uncertainty. He faces horrible losses. Yet he grows through suffering, maintains faith against all odds, and embraces the unspeakable beauty and goodness of human relationships. He is wise and generous, but never at the expense of honesty.

He writes as a Christian who truly understands the call and cost of discipleship. He aims through it all to pursue a life of faith, hope, and love. In short, of living as a Christian who trusts that God is *his* God. God is true to his promises and somehow provides a way through darkness and hardship.

I cannot tell you how much I learned. I knew a little about his story. I realized upon reading Eddie's book how little I really knew, not only about Eddie's own story but also about larger cultural issues, which he somehow manages to weave together into a seamless whole. I knew little about what is demanded to move through the maze of immigration, what is required to battle one crisis after another, what it means to remain committed to the gospel in the face of difficulty.

Eddie's story reminded me of how Christians—so very many of them over the centuries—have lived as exiles and pilgrims in this world, setting their sight on their true homeland, which is the kingdom of God. "All of these died in faith without having received the promises, but from a distance they saw and greeted them. They confessed that they were strangers and foreigners on the earth, for people who speak in this way make it clear that they are seeking a homeland. If they had been thinking of the land that they had left behind, they would have had opportunity to return. But as it is, they desire a better homeland, that is, a heavenly one. Therefore God is not ashamed to be called their God; indeed, he has prepared a city for them" (Hebrews 11:13-16).

Eddie's story could be added to Hebrews 11.

Finally, I learned a great deal about being an American. We have reason to celebrate the strengths and triumphs of this nation of ours. But not every moment and decision deserves unqualified praise. The nation has failed, too, as all nations do. I was reminded, as I often am these days, that no nation perfectly embodies the kingdom. Eddie's pilgrimage demonstrates how important and necessary it is for Christians to identify themselves first as disciples of Jesus and citizens of his kingdom.

There is much goodness in this book. Eddie himself models goodness. So do many others who appear in this book who exhibited the love of Christ to Eddie, especially his beloved wife, his in-laws, and close friends. Eddie belongs to the worldwide body of Christ. His story summoned me to renew my commitment to that body and to the gospel that serves as its foundation.

I commend this book to you. It tells a good story. But it does so much more. It awakens curiosity, touches the heart, and expands the mind. It also calls forth faith. It certainly did that to me.

Back to my family's summer in Africa. I did run in the mornings alongside giraffe and oryx. On clear days I climbed a hill overlooking the campus to gaze upon Mt. Kenya and Mt. Kilimanjaro off in the distance. I ate delicious African food with students on campus. I enjoyed many lively conversations.

But the most priceless experience was meeting and befriending Eddie Tokpa. I am glad that you, the reader, can come to know him, too. I trust you will be as enriched as I was, and have continued to be.

Gerald L. Sittser

Professor Emeritus of Theology, Whitworth University and author of nine books, including *A Grace Disguised*

Acknowledgments

While writing can be a lonely venture, a book is never the product of a single individual. During the process of writing *Faith and Resilience: A Refugee's Journey to Peace,* I have benefited from the generosity and support of many people and institutions. They are too many to name here, but for the sake of brevity, I want to acknowledge and thank those who have had the most significant impact on the success of this book.

First, I am immeasurably grateful to Illumify for their astonishing work in publishing this book. Thanks to everyone on the Illumify publishing team who helped me so much. Special thanks to Geoffrey Stone the editorial director, Jen Clark, my amazing book shepherd and operations director, and Debbie Lewis, the greatest cover designer I could ever imagine.

I want to thank my wife, Lisa! None of this would have been possible without her support and encouragement. Lisa, you are my number one cheerleader and encourager, and you have stood by me during my darkest times and all my successes. You were the first person who told me to write my story and made all the sacrifices to ensure it came to fruition. You consistently told me it was possible and that I should not give up. You are my forever true friend and partner. You inspire me daily with your incredible thoughtfulness, care for the people around you, and devotion to being as Christ-like as possible. A lifelong partner makes both the journey and destination worthwhile. Thank you for doing that for me and loving and caring for our family.

To my son, Zeke, who is a continuous source of love and inspiration! I write this story for you; I want you to know my story, background, and the challenges I have encountered. As a result, you are my first audience. Mom constantly reminded me to write my story for you. Someday, you will be old enough to start reading and learning more about the history of your dad's birth country, family, and his escape from the war. No matter what happens, I will always be your affectionate Dad and a grandfather to your children. I love you, son!

To my deceased parents, thank you for encouraging me in all of my pursuits and inspiring me to follow my dreams at a very young age when life was so difficult. You sacrificed your life working for an organization that paid you $3.19 daily so your children could attend the company's school for free. I always knew you believed in me and wanted the best for me, even when you were angry about my mistakes. Thank you for teaching me to be resilient and determined in the hardship that life threw at you through your grueling work at Firestone Rubber Plantation. Thank you for teaching me the importance of loving and caring for people regardless of their background, tribe, and ethnicity. I hope you would be proud of me today, knowing I am living that out! RIP!

Thank you, Gary Baughman; you've become the dad I never had! Despite your many other engagements and activities, you took this project on with enthusiasm, dedication, and precision. You made the book significantly better than it would have been had I written it alone. You were the first person to review the draft of my manuscript and make it comprehensible. Thank you for being there for me/us in our time of need. You've gone above and beyond to care for us/me in my health crisis.

To my other family members, Mama Lisa (Carolyn Baughman), Rebekah Knight-Baughman, Darren Knight-Baughman, and Jonah Baughman, thank you all for inviting me into your spaces and lives and accepting me as part of the Baughman and the Knight-Baughman families. I am very grateful to you all for supporting the writing of this book and encouraging me to process my trauma through writing my story. Thank you also for celebrating every milestone in my life.

Thank you, Nate and Bitsat Bulcha; I owe a debt of gratitude to you for encouraging and supporting my effort in writing, agreeing to read through the manuscript, and editing the first draft of this book. You believed in me from the get-go when I told you my intention of writing my memoir, and you instantly said, "Do it."

Finally, my deepest gratitude goes to my editor, Rose Winters. I am truly grateful for your time and effort in reviewing and refining the content so meticulously. Your keen eye for grammar, spelling, and structure, coupled with your constructive feedback, have helped transform the book into a more polished and professional work.

Preface

On December 24, 1989, a date I would later call the "beginning of woes," Liberia was invaded by insurgents, resulting in fourteen years of anarchy and mayhem, ruining many lives. Whereas I had previously depended on my parents' care, love, empathy, and attention, during the war I was left heartbroken, separated from my parents and from every support system I had.

I lost the opportunity for education, had to escape from Liberia, and was forced to move into a refugee camp in Ghana. I vividly recall the experiences, suffering, and trauma I went through in my attempt to flee from my home; witnessing fighting and destruction; seeing violent acts directed at me and loved ones; leaving parents, friends, and possessions behind; being transported in a crowded ship, and eventually finding temporary respite in a country at peace.

I lived for eight years in a refugee camp in Ghana, where the main activity in the camp was trying to survive, living in constant fear of not knowing whether we would survive, or die trying. That sort of experience challenges your self-worth, and can lead to anxiety, depression, and low self-esteem. I was essentially exiled from my country for sixteen years, while the rebels destroyed my homeland.

For much of my life in exile, I dreamt of writing down my refugee narrative one day, but I was never able to find the words, the time, the resources, or the emotional resiliency to truly express the suffering and the struggles I and many others endured during those years. Everything I tried to write about myself just oversimplified the complexity of the grief, struggle, and trauma I had experienced.

Dismantling the trauma of that experience, and restoring my sense of self, required difficult emotional effort, and the journey of writing this book has been healing. I am often asked, "How did you survive all that? How did you get so lucky to go to school when so many children wanted that opportunity but could not get it?" I cannot explain that except to say it was God's divine intervention in providing for me. Not to say that I was special to be chosen by God, but rather in His infinite character, he decided to be merciful to me and open doors for me to enter. I grabbed hold of the opportunities and never looked back.

I have met God in my pain, and He has stood with me in every circumstance. I found myself escaping from war, surviving a refugee camp, seeking education, immigrating to the US, raising a family, and dealing with cancer. God has always been near me and meeting my every need.

On many occasions, I considered throwing in the towel and giving up, but I always believed in God's reliability, word, ability, and strength to get me through my challenges. God was the pilot navigating my journey and bringing people in my path to support me.

I believe sharing my experiences can empower others who face challenges and setbacks and who can discover that education is a key to transforming one's life, breaking free from societal constraints, and charting one's own path. My journey exemplifies the resilience and determination of survivors. It shows that through the empowerment of education, one can break the cycle of poverty and provide a path toward a brighter future. If you seize every opportunity, no one and nothing can hinder you from achieving your goals.

———

As of this book's writing, I am still undergoing cancer treatment. The story in this book is about a boy living in a refugee camp and escaping a violent civil war, and about a man who has faced adversity and has struggled to face many life challenges.

The world seems to be lurching from one crisis to another—a global pandemic, economic uncertainty, political and social turmoil, and an array of natural disasters. Many people are experiencing personal trauma, declining health, unemployment, divorce, violent crime, or tragic accidents. Living through difficult times can take a heavy toll on your mood, health, and outlook, and it can leave you feeling helpless and overwhelmed by stress and anxiety—as it has for me these past three years while dealing with a chronic health crisis. Life is filled with difficulties, yet we can choose how we react to these challenges.

My memoir is for everyone who faces trauma and is struggling to cope, but you may also identify with my story if you are a refugee or asylum seeker living away from your place of birth. I hope my story inspires you to overcome the obstacles in your life because in an uncertain world, we need to rely on God by faith, and faith beckons us to be joyful in our trials and persevere amidst the challenges. No matter what you are going through, you have all the power and strength to weather any storm. Don't ever give up on yourself!

So, I send this book out with a prayer that it will bear light and truth, provide encouragement and comfort, and help readers develop a spirit of resilience to face an uncertain future knowing that God is with us.

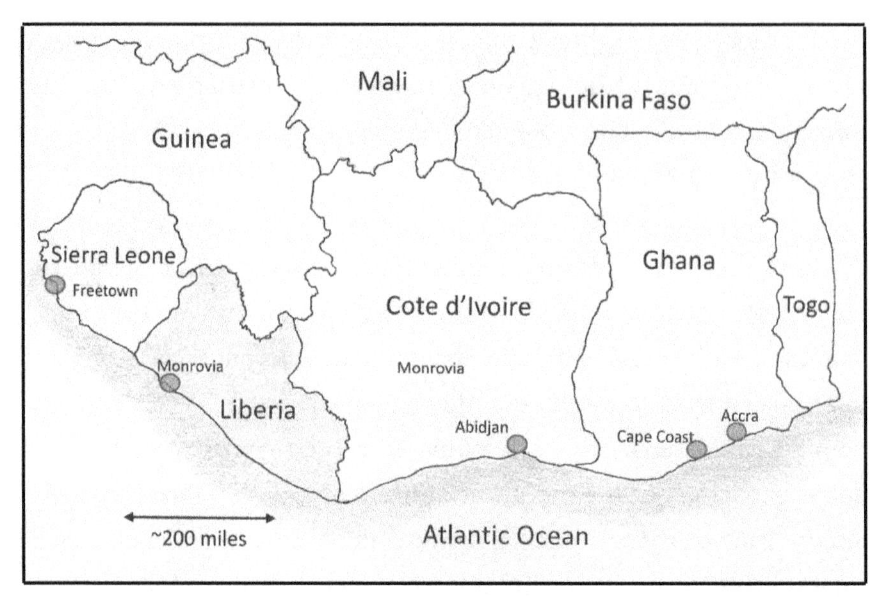

Map of West Africa

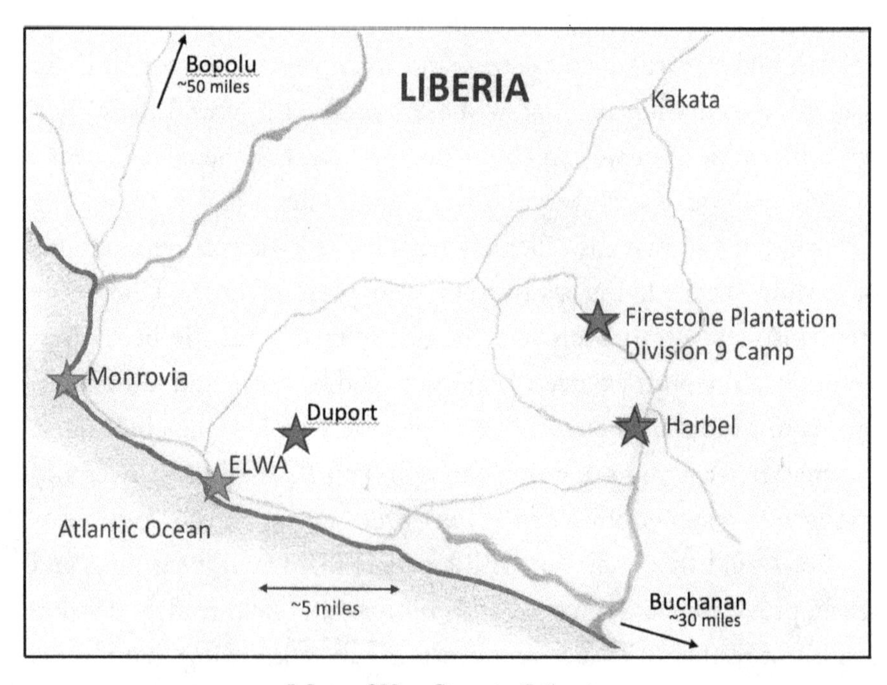

Map of Key Sites in Liberia

Introduction

A civil war forces a 17-year-old boy to flee his home, and he finds himself in an encampment packed with people, tents, tall grass, and very little food. He stands in line for hours simply to get a cup of millet porridge and a slice of bread. For many years the boy lives in constant fear and poverty in a strange country, experiencing displacement, the loss of a 'sense of place,' and an 'identity crisis.' The upheaval of war disrupts his education and social environment, and separates him from his family. He experiences a constant struggle for food, a sense of powerlessness, and a total lack of control over his situation, while waiting for the conflict in his homeland to end.

That 17-year-old boy was me; I fled the war in Liberia in 1990 and escaped to Ghana on a ship. I spent three days at sea without food or water, and I lived in an overcrowded refugee camp for eight years, constantly experiencing competition for food, a lack of water, a lack of sanitary facilities, and limited medical care. I was overcome with feelings of hopelessness, anxiety and fear and I saw abhorrent forms of violence, including sexual violence. Imagine a life where you are not heard or seen, a life trapped in limbo without any foreseeable end, living in a makeshift structure, unsanitary conditions, and struggling for your daily survival. Given the misery that such an encampment inflicts, it is essential that those who have experienced and endured that life tell their stories.

1
Liberian Conflict: A Brief History

Liberia's struggle for freedom and democracy began in 1822 when the American Colonization Society (ACS) founded the colony as a settlement for freed slaves from the United States. Since then, Liberia has struggled to find her identity. The True Whig Party (TWP), founded in 1869, was one of the oldest political parties in the world and the oldest in Africa,[1] and it held power continuously from 1877 until the coup in 1980. This ruling government consisted of the descendants of American slaves who had settled in the land known as Liberia ("the land of the free") but, as the land was already populated by the indigenous people, these descendants made up only one percent of the total population as of the 1962 census.[2]

The TWP government had a firm grasp on the reins of political and economic control. They held the lion's share of domestically owned wealth, and they maintained and vigorously applied certain aspects of their Western culture. This minority group ruled the country with an iron fist and seemingly limitless power. President William Tubman (1947-1971) and President William Tolbert

(1971-1980) combined to rule Liberia for thirty-three years, and Americo-Liberians constituted the majority of ministers in both administrations. During this period, a growing number of indigenous students in the Liberian institutions of higher education began demonstrating hostility towards the government, the most dramatic opposition coming from students at the University of Liberia. These pockets of discontent exposed the government's weaknesses and were a harbinger of even greater unrest.

The struggles began to intensify when I was just fifteen years old. On April 14, 1979, the price of rice suddenly increased from $22 to $25 per 100 pounds, resulting in upheaval that came to be known as the "Rice Riot." This price increase was the proverbial straw that broke the camel's back, unleashing twenty-five years of violence, mayhem, anarchy, death, and destruction in Liberia.

The Rice Riot was organized by the Progressive Alliance of Liberia (PAL), headed at the time by political activist Gabriel Baccus Matthews, who was able to harness the outrage of the people. The stated intent of the price increase had been to buttress Liberian farmers' efforts to maximize production and to increase the economic viability of the nation's staple food producers, and although this might seem like a worthy purpose designed to help the Liberian farmers, ordinary Liberians needed help to afford the cost. Before this announcement, there was already an outcry over Liberia's high cost of living. So, increasing the price of rice was like adding fuel to the fire, and it worsened an already bad situation by increasing anger and hostility.

The top officers in the Liberian military were Americo-Liberians, but the lower ranks consisted primarily of indigenous people, a composition that made the forces an ineffective instrument for maintaining law and order. When the Rice Riot began, soldiers quickly joined the demonstrators in the looting of shops and supermarkets rather than attempting to quell the protests. President Tolbert, realizing that the rioting was increasing, requested that the neighboring country of Guinea send in troops to help disperse the rioters and return the country to normalcy.

Since that fateful day, some political activists and observers of political events in Liberia have described the event as the most turbulent in the annals of Liberian history. It was the Tolbert regime's determination to suppress the Liberian opposition that triggered the coup. The mass arrests of civilian opposition elements had led to growing protests, which in turn caused the government to take up a stronger confrontational stance. With all of this heading toward a violent collision, a coup was triggered by the arrest of soldiers who had participated in the riot, further creating a general atmosphere of destabilization.

Sadly, a year later, on April 12, 1980, a bloody coup was staged by seventeen non-commissioned officers of the Armed Forces of Liberia (AFL), led by Samuel K. Doe, to overthrow the True Whig Party (TWP) of William R. Tolbert. Four days later, loyalists of Tolbert's government carried out an alleged revolt to remove the military, but they were defeated, and Doe was now in complete control.

Doe ordered all cabinet ministers in Tolbert's government to report themselves, and on April 22, 1980, Liberia's most powerful and economically potent leaders were tied to light poles and executed by a firing squad on a beach in Monrovia.

Soon after the coup, opinions were expressed from all sides of the Liberian political spectrum, including the young and older generations, which pointed to the fact that change had finally come in Liberia. Liberians welcomed the news of this bloody coup with jubilation and dancing, signifying that change had come and that indigenous Liberians had secured the right to assemble and protest against the government of the Americo-Liberians.

Sergeant Samuel K. Doe quickly moved to give reasons for the coup, and thousands demonstrated their support in Monrovia. His reasons were hardly different than those offered for coups in other parts of Africa. As Doe stated, they included the government's neglect of the Liberian poor, rampant corruption, detentions and convictions without trial of opposition politicians, a high rate of unemployment, the skyrocketing cost of living, and dreadful healthcare. Doe, an unknown Army sergeant prior to the coup, had no ideological inclinations. His first task was the cleansing of the most glaring social ills in Liberia, but it soon became clear that he had no idea of the direction he should take. Doe then moved to invite some Americo-Liberians to serve in his government. While many Americo-Liberians had fled the country in the wake of the takeover, others threw in their lot with Doe, seeking the chance for personal advancement in the new government. Doe established his government, naming it the "People's Redemption Council" (PRC). The PRC leaders introduced a new phrase that became famous in the Liberian political lexicon: "In the cause of the people, the struggle continues."

While the Doe cabinet was made up primarily of those who had endorsed his regime change, he also invited into the government returnees like Charles Taylor, and other political activists with American education such as Ellen Johnson-Sirleaf, Gabriel Baccus Matthews, and others. The PRC initially had a very hardline and radical tone to it—building the economy, attacking the problem of corruption in Liberian society, and solving the unemployment crisis by opening the door for investors to come into the country. Many thought that Liberia would never be the same again after April 12, 1980, but those from other indigenous groups who had hoped that change would benefit them were soon disappointed.

Those involved in the coup, having tasted power, sounded a clarion call to Liberians, that they were prepared to stay and lead the nation and its people to prosperity through a sound democratic process. The long-hoped-for indigenous Liberian revolution quickly dissolved after Doe failed to hand over power to a civilian government as he had pledged. Soon, pockets of discontent started to build within the military. There were several military coup attempts and as a result, Doe surrounded himself with his tribal men and women, while eliminating other indigenous tribal groups in the military and in government that he alleged opposed his regime.

In 1985, Doe announced his intention to run for President and created the National Democratic Party of Liberia (NDPL). In the same year, highly politically contested presidential and general elections were held, but they were manipulated, and the results were well-masterminded and rigged in favor of Doe and the NDPL. Doe followed a pattern of oppression and human rights violations, both during the period of military rule and after he assumed the civilian presidency. His regime was characterized by the ruthless suppression of any perceived threat to his power.

Doe's methods of governance helped set the stage for the violent civil wars that later engulfed the country. The human rights violations perpetrated by Doe's PRC military government and his NDPL civilian government were another step on Liberia's path to civil war. It is important to note that the culture of brutality and impunity, as well as the increasing ethnic conflict, was a harbinger of the crisis to come.

Making matters worse in Liberia, Charles Taylor, who was the Director General of the General Services Agency (GSA) in charge of purchasing for the Liberian government, was sacked in May 1983 for embezzling money. Taylor and many other politicians fled the country and went into exile, thus starting a new chapter in the struggle for freedom. In my view, the battle still continues today because unemployment and the price of rice, for which the former President William R. Tolbert was made the sacrificial lamb in the bloody military coup of April 12, 1980, are still relatively high.

Children and youth are believed to thrive in stable and nurturing environments, the benefits of which extend across various developmental and health outcomes. Unfortunately, this was not the case for me and many children in Liberia. I grew up in an environment characterized by unpredictability, hardship, conflict, instability, and uncertainty. These environments also had a profound influence on my behavior, such as aggression and defiance and a burning desire to get out of Firestone's neocolonialism reimposition of imperialist control of its employees.

The struggle is not just *my* story or experience, but a story and experience of an entire country still trying to rise from the ashes of its past. A story that exposes what it looks like to be completely stripped of everything you have ever known—your family, school, possessions, job, and money and yet, still have the faith to forge ahead. Through my eyes as a fifteen-year-old boy, I will endeavor to narrate my struggles and experiences in the fourteen years of civil war that claimed the lives of tens of thousands of people. So, voyage with me amid adversity, trials, and triumph. Let's begin from the beginning: the Firestone Rubber Plantation where I was born and grew up.

2
Dawn on the Plantation

"Hope is being able to see that there is light despite all of the darkness"

—Desmond Tutu

I woke up slowly, my eyes adjusting to the dark. The coolness of the early morning air permeated our small, one-room hut on the Firestone Rubber Plantation. I could hear my father outside, in the outdoor kitchen he'd built next to the house, and I could make out my mother getting ready for the day in the pre-dawn darkness. It was about 4:00 a.m., I judged, knowing that my father habitually rose around this time daily.

I sat up, stretched my stiff limbs, stood up, and walked out the door. I picked up a bucket from the kitchen and mumbled to my father a sleepy greeting. Passing the extension on the side of the building, I thought about my brother, who had moved out of the house just a year before to live with his friends. My sister was probably in the extension now, still sleeping. I continued to the pit latrine, just a short distance from our home, about three minutes away.

After using our rudimentary community toilet, I continued to the creek with my empty bucket, swinging it as I walked. A slight mist rose from the river, and down a small hill to the shore I filled my pail with the cool water, balancing my feet on the rocks as I did so. The water flowed fast, and the bucket was easy to fill. Everyone in our area used the creek for drinking water and had done so for years. I lifted the bucket out of the water and began the slow journey back to the hut with the water.

On my return to our hut, I saw other boys my age also getting ready to join their fathers in collecting the latex from the rubber trees. Together we would all return home in time to begin the long journey to school for the afternoon. Our days were long, and our nights were short, but we knew we were fortunate. Not only did our parents remind us that they were working hard so we could go to the plantation school without tuition, but we were told that if we dedicated ourselves to our studies, we might be able to find jobs outside of the plantation someday, or we could be the superintendent at the plantation. We lived in poverty, but so did most people in Liberia, especially at the Firestone Rubber Plantation.

My friends and I lived with our parents in similar huts — small, made of mud, and built by a man whose name was only legend to me: Harvey Firestone. In 1926, Mr. Firestone had signed a ninety-nine-year lease with the government of Liberia for rubber farming. He'd planted rubber trees on the one million acres of land that he'd leased from the government, and he'd promptly built small mud huts for his employees to live in while they worked for him. By the time my parents moved into our hut and had three children, the rudimentary homes had been previously used for fifty years by families similar to ours. You can imagine the condition of that house. The roof leaked when it rained, the walls were cracked, and it was pretty dilapidated.

How strange that this man, about whom I knew so little, would have such a significant impact on my life. It was *his* home I lived in, *his* trees I tapped with my father, *his* school I attended, and *his* river I played in. The Firestone family owned one million acres in Liberia, and the 14,000 employees who worked there were almost frozen in time, living the same way they had lived since 1926. Though Firestone did not employ children directly, it set high daily production quotas for its employees that could only be made with extra help. To meet their quotas, employees could hire others as subcontractors whom they would pay from their trifling wages. But alternatively, they could get their wives or children to help them at no monetary cost. Thus, I and many children on the plantation were involved in the daunting task of tapping rubber. It is worth mentioning that rubber tappers at Firestone were paid based on their productivity. A daily wage for an employee was $3.19[3]. If an employee did not meet the daily quota, he would earn only half of his daily wage, which was why tappers hired subcontractors or got the support of their families to help meet the daily quotas.

If my father didn't tap his 750 trees daily, he would not earn his daily paycheck of $3.19. Besides latex production, he was also required to apply chemicals (both fungicides and fertilizer) to the trees for protection and to increase production. In addition, he was also required to "under-brush" the trees he tapped. In addition to these low wages per day, there was also a wage deduction from each tapper's wages. Deductions were typically for things like a compulsory bag of rice, which cost $34, a can of sardines, luncheon meat (Spam), a bag of salt, a bar of laundry soap, a liter of kerosene, and a gallon of vegetable oil. The more supplies you received, the lower your salary during payday.

When I returned to our hut, I found the 'col bowl' I had left the day before and heated it in our small outdoor kitchen. A 'col bowl' is a Liberian term meaning leftover food from a previous meal not eaten but kept till the next day. The meager leftovers in the col bowl were just enough to fill my stomach so that I could work until just after noon. My father did the same, and when we were finished, we set off to begin tapping.

Tapping rubber trees was a labor-intensive job. It started with cleaning the land, caring for the nursery of the rubber trees, and weeding and pruning fields and young trees—all integral elements in the production process. The most labor-intensive stage, however, was the tapping of trees. This involved each tree being 'tapped' using a V-groove knife, with a cup attached to the tree just below the cut made in the tree's bark to collect the latex. On a normal working day, tappers would collect 'cup lumps' from the previous day—that is, the latex that had poured into the cup overnight—then clean the cup, tap the tree again, and return to collect the new latex later that same day. At the end of the day (or alternately after a whole field had been cleared), the tapper would carry the fresh latex and cup lumps to the nearest field station for weighing.

Ammonia was added to the latex at the field station as the first step in producing rubber. At this stage, there were safety concerns for workers during the collection and production process, with injuries in the field including eye and skin damage from spilling latex, snake bites, back pain and muscle cramps from carrying heavy loads to the field stations, and exposure to the ammonia that was added to the latex at the field station. No wonder my father would complain of back pain and muscle aches constantly. It was not a surprise, given that working as a tapper was hard physical labor, involving carrying loads weighing up to 150 pounds. Cases of back pain were common among workers. Skin infections were another common concern. There were also work-related accidents, mainly resulting from blade wounds received while cutting the bush with a machete or tapping the tree with a V-groove knife, as well as wounds and infections caused by hot rubber getting on the skin.

Latex was collected and sent from the field station to Harbel at the larger processing plant for further treatment and prepared for shipment to the United States, where the rubber was manufactured, and the finished products were shipped back to Liberia as commodities. Today, Liberia remains an exporter of raw rubber (a relatively low-value commodity) and has no secondary or tertiary rubber processing factory. While tire manufacturing in Liberia has been discussed for decades, neither Firestone nor the Liberian government has initiated building a rubber processing and manufacturing factory for tires or any rubber products. The Government's failure to hold Firestone accountable and ensure that it takes responsibility for violating labor laws and exploiting the country's resources has enabled the Firestone Plantation in Liberia to avoid following the rules in dealing with workers and investing in the country.

On any given day, I would set off for the plantation and get to work. I would shear off a thin layer of the rubber tree's bark, conscious that if I cut too deeply it would injure the tree, but also very mindful when peeling the bark to prevent the ammonia and sulfuric acid from going into my eyes or pouring onto my skin. Once I had made the incision, I could put a small spigot into the hole and attach a cup below with a wire. I could count on the tree flowing until early afternoon when my father would return to collect the liquid.

Having tapped the tree, I would focus on the necessary maintenance tasks. I would apply fungicide to the tree for protection and fertilizer for increased yield and remove the brush from under the tree. Satisfied with my work, I would move on to the next tree, aware of the hundreds of trees I had yet to tap before returning to our hut for the food my mother was no doubt preparing. My father would be a few yards away at another tree. He would be back in the area in the afternoon, and he would have to finish without me.

His clothes were tattered, and his shoulders were covered in red blisters from carrying buckets full of raw latex suspended from an iron pole to the processing plant two miles from the tapping site. At the processing site, I would see my father sitting perched like a statue, surrounded by green shrubbery and tall, eerie, splotched rubber trees. At the processing site, we were welcomed by an awful stench, which I can only compare to the smell of rotten eggs or cheese. Not just ordinary rotten eggs, but the kind that had been reeking for weeks. That is what latex smelled like when it was being processed. This toxic smell posed a health hazard for the workers and caused workers and their subcontractor workers to get sick.

Concerning common types of sicknesses, the leading cause of illness and death at Firestone Rubber Plantation was malaria and diarrhea. Firestone did not distribute mosquito nets to employees. I myself was constantly infected almost every other week because we did not have a mosquito net. It usually started with severe fever and chills. Soon, I could not walk, and I would retreat into my bed, soaking several layers of bedsheets and suffering excruciating pain that felt like pins and needles coursing through my body. The clinic was far from the camp and not easily accessible to company employees and their families. My mama would usually take charge as my 'nurse' to treat me with African medicinal herbs, giving me pepper soup to drink, believing that it would make me sweat, thus "releasing" malaria from my body through the sweat.

Paternalism was evidenced at the Firestone Rubber Plantation by a pattern of gift-giving from a more powerful entity, in this case, Firestone, to a lower status group (the Firestone rubber tappers) consistent with a system designed to maintain a privileged position. For example, Firestone claimed that its food subsidies, healthcare, and "free education system" that were given to Liberian workers—who tapped rubber up to twenty-one hours a day—was all that they needed. But in reality, the company exploited their labor and controlled their lives. White supremacy and segregation underpinned Firestone's pursuit of profit in Liberia, manifested in how employees were treated. White employees from the US lived in very nice houses built near a beautiful golf course and drove fancy cars, and their kids went to a private school in Monrovia. In contrast, the workers lived in dilapidated houses. And sometimes the white employees described Liberia as "a child of the United States" because freed slaves from America founded the country, named it Liberia, the "land of the free." And they called its capital Monrovia in honor of James Monroe, the fifth president of the United States whom it is believed procured US government money for the project. And they went on to establish the US dollar as the national currency.

One day, we worked for hours in the early morning dark, mostly in silence. After some time, the sun rose and its glow started warming the trees and my body. Now we could see a slight mist coming off the plants and could work slightly faster, our fingers not fumbling for our equipment. The only drawback to the sun was the assurance that the latex would be slower to flow, and the trees would be more reluctant to yield the quota my father needed to reach.

In some ways, tapping became a rhythm after the sun came up: shear the barks, insert the spigot, attach the cup, clear the brush, spray the tree. And again: shear, insert, attach, clear, spray. But this monotony was needed to make producing more latex from the tree easier.

My nose burned with the putrid smell of the chemical used in the latex and my eyes stung from exposure to the maintenance chemicals.

Though rough from the work, my hands would get pricked from time to time. Looking back, I realize that this was not a work fit for children, but we had no choice — my family had to eat. Rather than wearing masks to protect his nose from the assault, my father and other plantation workers just ingested the foul stench day in and day out. It took all my willpower not to retch whenever I was at the processing site. However, the rancid stench was the least of my father's worries. He worried that he needed to make enough money to save for our schooling.

At last, father told me we were finished for the day, and we returned to the road, exhausted. My stomach didn't feel empty despite the lack of food, but my feet felt heavy, and my steps were slow. We trudged back home, where my mother was preparing our only meal for the day. I would save some of my portions for the next morning's col bowl, so it was good that I didn't feel too hungry on this day.

When we returned to the hut, my mother was around the side of the fire. She had used most of the water I'd brought up the hill that morning, and the firewood pile was almost gone. I cursed silently — I would have to go out again for firewood after school. My mood did not brighten when I realized what time it was — we had been out too long. I spooned the meal into my bowl and ate two-thirds of it as quickly as possible, even though I knew it would hurt my stomach to eat so quickly. After a thank you to my mother between bites and carefully covering my bowl for the morning, I ran out the front door and slowed to a fast walk when I reached the road. I wanted to be at school on time.

Walking to school took just under two hours, and having left late, I knew my friends were well ahead of me. I walked quickly, hearing my pants swish with each step. As I was walking fast to catch up with my friends, I reflected on the conditions that my father was trapped in on the plantation. We eventually reached the school campus but were nearly thirty minutes late. Just a few meters away from entering the compound, the principal saw us in the distance and yelled, "Come here!" At that point, my friends and I knew we were in trouble. We looked at each other, wondering whether we should escape into the bushes and go back home, as many students would normally do to escape the harsh punishment. Immediately, two of my friends escaped, and I was left standing there with my bowlegged friend, who could barely run.

When we reached the principal, I was hauled to the front of the class and told to pull my shirt tail up to my waist to show my buttocks for better impact of the cane (whip). I nurtured a faint hope that I would be spared. I took a backward glance at my classmates. The look on most of their faces was shock, incredulity, and discomfort. I turned back to face the wall and managed to catch the eye of the principal, who seemed to be relishing the moment. The first five lashes didn't hurt so much. Over the next ten, I started squirming and writhing in pain. It was humiliating enough to be beaten in front of the class, but it would be even worse to cry in front of your friends and classmates. But by the seventeenth stroke, my will broke, and I could barely hold still. I couldn't contain the tears that streaked down my cheeks. I screamed for mercy. I was afforded none. I received all twenty-five lashes in front of my classmates. Not long afterward, school was over for that day, and we started our walk back home.

On that day, I was brutally humiliated before my friends and classmates, and it was so hard to learn in that space which held so many memories for me, memories of shame, anger, and humiliation. But this type of discipline was not new to me. My father had two ways to affect a desired behavior in me as a child. One was withholding food from me, which was our only meal for the day, and the other was physical punishment, such as flogging. I received both of these punishments in our house, but most frequently the rod was used as a tool for punishment and an instrument to direct my path.

On typical mornings, the sun filtered through the rubber trees as I walked to school. Butterflies flitted between the rubber trees and our grubby group of ramblers on the road. But at night, I lay on my bed, my eyes still open even though the dark permeated the room, and I thought about all the days to come; monotonous and rugged but dependable. I thought about my brother, who would probably eventually work for Firestone himself, and my sister, who was spending much time with her boyfriend, who also lived on the plantation. Somehow, I sensed that there was something beyond Firestone for me. I resolved that I would continue to help my father to work and keep attending school so that I could walk away at some point.

For me, this was a resolution I had to repeat to myself to keep. It would be easy to stay at Firestone. The work was steady and reliable. The people were familiar, and we shared food and what meager resources we had with one another. The living conditions were deplorable, and life was a constant struggle. There was a time when I felt utterly stuck. The sun rose with new and limitless opportunities, but everything felt the same as it set. The day was new, but the issues and the struggles were old. I felt imprisoned no matter how much positive thinking and attitude changing I did. My environment was the same. The feelings of hopelessness and frustration were the same. Have you ever felt stuck like that? No matter what you try, everything seems to make little difference. This is the waiting period, where we linger until divine timing permits us to move forward. It might sound dramatic, but these seasons can feel like a prison. You are doing everything right. But you feel trapped in the system. But know this: grit and perseverance help us to develop the ability to wait. They help shape the way we behave while we're waiting. It was almost beyond my comprehension that it was possible to leave.

When I finally did leave, years later, it was reported that Firestone and Bridgestone had merged, and Bridgestone Corporation purchased Firestone-Liberia, transforming the companies' combined operation into the largest tire and rubber company. Today, Firestone-Liberia is a subsidiary of Bridgestone. The internal and external pressure that Firestone-Liberia encountered regarding its operations has led to changes in its operations and engagements with workers. Houses are being rebuilt, there are several primary schools on the plantation, and today, there is a high school on the plantation. In 2007, the first free and fair union elections were held in the plantation's history. Nonetheless, despite these positive recent developments, there is still a need for sustained action to ensure that Firestone Liberia and its parent company, Bridgestone, honor their commitments to human rights, labor rights, and environmental sustainability for an engaged civil society to ensure that Firestone stays accountable.

3
A Journey to Freedom: A Start to a Lifetime of Hope

"If you want something you have never had, you must be willing to do something you have never done."

—Thomas Jefferson

I stood eyeing myself in the mirror before making the journey to Monrovia to start a new chapter of my life. I felt euphoric over the idea that I was leaving Firestone to visit my aunt and uncle, Bindu and George, in Monrovia. At the same time, I was very fearful and frightened by the idea of leaving Papa and Mama, my friends, and the only community I had known. Nevertheless, something inside me was telling me that this trip would change the course of my life.

Bindu came to Firestone to get me. It was a big deal for me. I had never before left Papa and Mama's hut in Firestone. The only town I had ever known, apart from the Firestone Plantation camp, was Harbel, a town where the rubber was collected for export. I was determined to venture beyond the plantation and view the rest of the world.

"Do I look okay?" I asked my friend, David.

"Look fine to me," David said.

I sat, perched like a statue, surrounded by camp friends who had heard the news that I was leaving and had run to come to say goodbye. But I was also surrounded by shrubbery and tall, eerie, splotched rubber trees, and they were a clear reminder again that I needed to make the trip. Emotions became more frayed as Bindu and I set off to leave the camp, the place I had known to be our village, the place affectionately known by many as "The Plantation."

We trekked down the dusty road for twenty minutes or so, to get the only public transport that normally traveled on that route, a minivan or taxicab. We boarded a rusty taxicab crammed with six passengers to Harbel, our next stop to change vehicles. It is important to note that taxi cabs in Liberia are small and usually crammed with six passengers at a time, four in the back seat and three in the front seat, including the driver, which leaves passengers squeezing against each other and vulnerable to being robbed. There were also motorcycle taxis known as "pen-pens," a name that comes from the sound of their constant horn blowing.

From Harbel, we took another taxicab to Smell No Taste, a famous town between Roberts International Airport (RIA) and the infamous Firestone Plantation. This town got its name when the American Air Force base in the town filled the community with its wafting fragrances of cooking food that the locals could smell but never taste. The taxi park at Smell No Taste was chaotic, with noise of taxi touts (conductors calling out to people, asking if they require transport) and the shouts of vendors in every corner of the park. Passengers were wandering from one taxi stage to another, looking for taxis to their destinations. It was an exciting place, and it was easy for people to get robbed because of the congestion. There, we got a cab to our final destination, Monrovia.

We started our last leg of the journey and were joined by other passengers. As we drove, I craned my neck, looking through the window attempting to catch a glimpse of the Atlantic Ocean, but I did not see it.

We made our way to Bindu and George's. "Welcome!" George said. "How was the drive?" I smiled and said it was good, and that I had seen an airplane for the very first time. Bindu then took me into my room and showed me my bed. It was a two-bedroom house with a kitchen. That night I lay in my bed staring at the ceiling, anticipating the daylight so that I could go see the city.

The next day, Bindu and George gave me a full orientation about city life, including the 'dos and don'ts' as well as their house rules. One of my responsibilities in the house was to do laundry every Saturday and mop the house. During our meeting, they never discussed anything about me starting school or if that was even possible. Of course, I was not courageous enough to say anything about it.

I spent my first two months living with Bindu and George as a domestic worker, hoping that it would work out for me to start school. My work at home became so hard that I almost wanted to leave Monrovia to return to Firestone. I washed clothes, not with soap powder, like they have in America, but with a blue bar of soap on a washboard— a tool designed for hand washing clothing, usually constructed with a rectangular wooden frame in which are mounted a series of ridges or corrugations for the clothing to be rubbed upon. Sometimes, my best friend, Jerry, who was also living with his uncle in the neighborhood, would come to help me wash those clothes. On Saturday, I washed them and put them in the sun to dry. At the end of the day, I took any damp clothes into my room and put them back in the sun the next morning. Another house rule was to wash every dirty dish before bed to prevent cockroaches from infesting the house. At night, mosquitoes would fight to take over my room, and I did not have a mosquito net.

One day, Bindu told me she would take me to the beach to see the ocean. I was extremely excited! I was looking forward to the weekend; it couldn't come fast enough. The day finally came, and we went to the beach. I stood there completely still and stared in total awe. "How could water be so vast?" I asked. "Vast" is a word far too small to describe how magnificent and breathtaking the ocean was. I could not help but gaze into the immensity of it.

I yelled to Jerry, as a wave came splashing. He laughed at me so hard, saying, "Look at this 'village boy.'" Yes, I was from the village but to be called a "village boy" or "native boy" was used as an insult or a degrading term for filth. Conversely, it reminded me that poverty and ill-being are the lack of material possessions, insecurity, social isolation, lack of opportunity, and lack of freedom of choice and action, which is why I could work as a house boy with no control over my life. I sometimes believed that poverty was a crime that my parents committed, which was still haunting me. I did not believe I would ever get out of such a situation.

Having been born and raised in the village, seeing an ocean for the first time was an over-the-moon experience. I admired the sheer beauty of it; I was amazed at how wide it spread to the horizon and how the big ships looked as if they were touching the sky. I loved the feel of a cool breeze blowing across my skin; I observed the beauty of waves running toward my feet, hitting one another, and taking up a different course.

Seeing the ocean was just another new experience I had among all the experiences of coming to a different environment. I didn't use a flush toilet in Firestone, I didn't use a spoon regularly, and I had to learn all about this new city life. I had to change my habit of eating with my hands and to practice the city etiquette.

Being away from my family and friends was daunting in many ways. For one thing, I felt alone and uncared for among the new people whom I was supposed to call family. There were mixed feelings of freedom, independence, nervousness, doubt, and confusion. But it was overshadowed by the confidence and anticipation of becoming a part of a new environment, learning new things, opening myself to greater possibilities, growing up, and becoming a better person.

The following weekend after the beach experience, I resumed my routine as a "houseboy" doing my usual tasks. Ms. Miatta (not her real name) was a next-door neighbor, amiable, caring, and compassionate. One Saturday morning, while I was washing clothes as usual, she looked through her kitchen window and told me she wanted to tell me something.

"Excuse me, Eddie," she shouted. "May I talk with you?"

"Yes, Ma," I responded. 'Ma' is a respectful and honorable word to address an elderly woman, a motherly figure, which is why the first female president in Liberia was affectionately known as "Ma Ellen." I walked up to her kitchen window, and she asked me how I had answered her. I told her, "I said I answered you, 'Yes, Ma.' This is how I was taught to answer the older ladies in the neighborhood in Firestone—that, or either 'auntie' or 'cousin.'" She told me not to refer to her as "Ma," "cousin," or "auntie," but instead, to use her name, Miatta. I did not ask her why she didn't want to be called those respectful names. I assumed she did not want to be seen as old.

She gave me a big plate of jollof rice with chicken. I was overjoyed. Just what I needed, because I was hungry. Jollof rice is a staple in West

African cuisine. It's made from rice, vegetables in a mild tomato curry sauce, onions, and chicken. It is scrumptious and very flavorful.

She asked, "Why are you doing this kind of God-forsaken work every Saturday morning?"

I laughed and said, "I have to do this to have the opportunity to go to school. And I must do this to have a place to stay in Monrovia."

"Don't you have any relatives to stay with and go to school?" she asked.

I told her that I was staying with family and the rest of my family lived in Firestone, but I would have to return to Firestone if I couldn't get into school soon. And besides, I didn't have the money to pay my tuition and the family had brought me here to work, to help pay my tuition.

As she was talking to me, I could see in her eyes that she was feeling sympathy for me and for the manner of work I was doing. I said, "Okay, let me go and finish my work."

She opened her purse and handed me twenty United States dollars! She said, "You can use that to buy something for yourself or use it as transportation when you are going to Firestone."

I stood there sobbing! Her kindness and generosity touched me so much that I cried even harder. I wanted a better life. I wanted never to have to go home to Firestone. I've often wished I could find her now and thank her for what she did that day. That act of kindness showed me that I matter. I was thrilled and surprised -- twenty dollars was a lot of money.

I went back to complete my laundry. I dreaded Saturdays because it was a day of never-ending chores. Saturday's cleaning was grueling on many levels. I was not too fond of it because I'd already worked all week, mopping the floor, washing dishes, and running errands. I needed more energy for Saturday's major cleaning and laundry.

After six months, I was not seeing any light at the end of the tunnel for me to be in school, so I decided to go back to visit Papa and Mama in Firestone, with the intent of not coming back to the city unless I was assured of going to school. I begged George and Bindu to allow me to go and see Papa and Mama, but they wanted me to stay until George got his salary in order to give me transport and buy some items to take to Papa and Mama. But I insisted that I wanted to go. They granted my request and luckily I still had the twenty dollars Miatta had given me.

I hopped down the three steps outside the house and gripped my suitcase, which was actually a plastic bag with all my clothes, and trekked for one and a half hours to downtown Monrovia (Water Street) to the minibus station where I boarded one of the minibuses to Harbel for five dollars. As I crossed the Farmington River that separated the Firestone Rubber Plantation and Roberts International Airport, I was welcomed by the ungodly stench as a reminder that I was back in Firestone.

The bus arrived in Harbel and I went to the local market, using ten of the remaining fifteen dollars to buy some food items for my mom. After shopping, I took a taxi, and within an hour's drive I was in the camp. Papa was not home, but Mama was there. She welcomed me and immediately started asking me questions. She asked, "How is the city? How are Bindu and her husband? Did you come to visit?"

"Yes, I came to visit," I responded, "But I am not planning to go back."

"Why?" she asked.

"I have not been in school since I got to Monrovia. I've just been doing housework and washing clothes a lot."

When Papa came home, Mama narrated the story to him and he said, "You will stay here and go to school. Maybe God will provide a scholarship for you."

He tried to cushion me with support, but this time, my commitment to life in Firestone was no longer there. What had appeared to be the start of a new beginning for me—the start of a life of hope and aspirations—was quashed, and I found myself back in Firestone going through the same routines.

I was tired of living in 'camps' and seeing my family trapped in poverty and working as enslaved people while the elites lived in the 'bungalows.' We were admittedly 'campers' because only tappers and service workers lived in the neighborhoods called camps. Those higher up in the company's hierarchy lived in bungalows, the word inherently implying houses with 24-hour electricity, running water, indoor plumbing, and with each employee being given a car. Their children also went to a good school, and they didn't have to walk to school—they were provided with a bus to pick each of them up from their houses and take them to school.

Unlike my dad, my mom was not an optimist. She hated our living conditions. She also knew our living conditions would never improve with the salary my dad was earning. In spite of all this, we tried to stay content, but the 'schooling' benefit frustrated me and Mom the most. Firestone always bragged about their workers' benefits and the fact that "even the tappers had access to free education, health insurance, and lived in housing units provided by the company." But our houses came with no electricity, no running water, and no indoor plumbing system, nor did they have enough room to accommodate a typical Liberian family of five or six children. Moreover, with such indecent salaries, my dad couldn't meet the requirement for my schooling.

I thought we were blessed, though, and I always told Mama this because they only had three children. What about the typical Liberian family who proudly had six, maybe ten children, and all had to live in a one-bedroom hut provided by Firestone? I was afraid of being trapped in Firestone like my brother. He lived in Firestone, got married there, and had ten children. When I saw him working like a slave to support his wife and ten children, I wanted to be educated. Every day, I was reminded that slavery isn't dead, it is manufactured in Firestone, and my dad was one of them as I saw him waking up at 4:00 a.m. to go for his tapping. So, Papa's optimism that life would improve for us living in Firestone angered me even more. He was not oblivious, so it frustrated me that he consistently faked happiness and insisted on staying positive.

That fueled every bad emotion within me because I knew the only way out of this poverty trap was education. So, on many occasions, I boycotted going to help my dad. Whenever that happened, he would use food as punishment. He would order my mom not to give me food, but Mama would hide food and give it to me to eat. Whenever I would boycott going to help my dad, I would walk to Harbel Hill Golf Course, where most of the elites and aristocracy of the Firestone Plantation played golf, and would serve as a caddie for any golfer who wanted help. This was my means of earning extra cash to support myself in junior high.

One day, as Mama was giving me food to eat after I'd rebelled and hadn't helped Papa, he saw her, and they got into an argument, resulting in a serious fight. This same argument resulted in additional fights. But you never get used to it. It was my fault, I thought to myself. They were fighting because of me. If only I had accepted the punishment and refused to accept the offer from Mama, they would not have fought.

At some point, I had to stop saying it was my fault and avoid blaming myself. Even if my parents sometimes argued and would argue 'about' me, I was not the cause of the dispute. I couldn't "make" them fight just as I couldn't "stop" them from fighting; they chose to do it because of the frustration of life, living in poverty, and working in a challenging environment to make ends meet. If I were not the reason, they would have still found something to argue about because of the frustration of living in Firestone. I got upset, angry, anxious, down, irritable, and stressed merely by living in Firestone. So, I resolved not to stay in Firestone but to seek opportunities elsewhere for my personal development, growth, and educational pursuits. I anticipated that day to come when I could leave, and that day finally came.

4
Point of No Return

"Every second that goes by is a point of no return"
—J. R. Rim

Life is like a river: it just goes up and down and around and around, and sometimes, it flows steadily. It has so many twists and turns that no one seems to know where it began or where it will end. The river will encounter obstacles and challenges and will change direction because of the obstacles encountered, but it will continue the journey to its goal. When one path is blocked, it seeks another path, and sometimes fresh water is added to the existing water. There are many parallels between the river and our lives, and my life can be likened to a flowing river. Just as I thought the river of my life had come to a dead end, fresh water was added.

I saw two white men walking into the camp with many children following them. I was just twelve years old at the time. Out of curiosity, I ran to see what was going on. It turned out that the two men were missionaries from ELWA, which stands for "Eternal Love

Winning Africa." They had come to share the Gospel with the residents of the camp. I was among twenty children following the two missionaries that afternoon. We gathered at a shelter designated for a community meeting and we sang a few Sunday School songs.

"The mountains are His; the rivers are His, the stars are His handiwork too." (Clap, clap). This part did not make sense to me because when I looked around me, I didn't see mountains, I only saw rubber trees. Did they belong to God too? The river, yes, because that was where we got our drinking water.

The last part of the song said: "My God is so big, so strong and so mighty, there's nothing my God cannot do for you!" I said to myself, "I want to try this God."

We also sang another song: "Jesus loves me, this I know, for the Bible tell me so." After singing, one of the missionaries, David Mai, told a Bible story about God loving the world and giving His son to die. He gave a simple compelling Sunday School invitation for us to accept Jesus. I was among several children who put up our hands to invite Jesus into our lives.

On September 25, 1985, I invited Jesus Christ to come into my life and take control, and I began my journey with Jesus Christ. I remember it as if it were yesterday! I was twelve years old, and I was in the camp attending the elementary school, which was a two-hour walk from the camp. Coming from a home that lacked the basic necessities of life, money was hard to come by, and Jesus was never spoken about in our house. I knew about God because Papa was a strong worshiper of Traditional African Religion (TAR), so I thought I should place my faith in him to help me in my situation. In the following week, I became convinced that this was the time for me to trust in Christ because the god my dad talked to had never helped us in our crisis. I believed that Jesus died for my sins on the cross, was buried, and rose on the third day as the Son of God. Acknowledging that I needed my sins to be forgiven, I prayed and called on the Lord Jesus to save me. And He did! I realized things would never be the same again.

I had not simply said a prayer or had an emotional experience—something radical had happened. I did not understand much, but I knew that I was different. I had begun to follow Jesus, and every Wednesday when the missionaries came to the camp, I would attend their Bible study.

I was growing spiritually, but I still did not trust God completely. I needed to be strengthened more. At one of our weekly Wednesday Bible Study meetings, David Mai began quizzing me on my Bible verses. Suddenly, he asked me, "Are you in school?"

"No," I answered, "I have finished junior high, but my parents don't have the money for me to go to high school."

Then he said, "There is a vocational school in Monrovia called Liberia Opportunity Industrialization Center (LOIC) that offers nine months training in various fields such as electrical, plumbing, carpentry, masonry, et cetera." He asked, "Have you heard about it?"

"I have not" I responded. He said that if I wanted to visit to get information about the school, he could help me get there. I went home and told Mama and Papa about my conversation with David Mai.

Mama was so happy, and she asked, "When are you going?"

I replied, "I don't know whether I should go because I don't have the money for school." Mama insisted, "You should go; you never know how God will use it to open other doors."

Wow! I could not believe it! But she had always supported me. I was reminded of Mark 9:23, "Everything is possible for one who believes." I did believe, but it seemed as if the Lord was saying to me, "O ye of little faith." My faith was getting stronger and stronger with each day that God allowed my eyes to open. I had already asked the Lord to guide me and open the door, but I also pleaded with God to close every door if He didn't want me to leave Firestone.

David Mai took me to ELWA, I spent the night at his house, and he drove me to LOIC the next morning to get the necessary information. I filled out the forms and returned them. A week later, I was informed that I had been accepted into the Carpentry Department. I leaped for joy much like the Ethiopian eunuch did after he was baptized (Acts 9:39). But that joy and happiness did not last very long because soon I began thinking about how I would pay for tuition and accommodations, as the school did not have a dormitory. When I told Mama and Papa that I was accepted into LOIC to do carpentry, they were happy... until I told them that I didn't have money for school, and, if I *did* get money, I still didn't have money for accommodations. That night, as a young Christian, I went to God in prayer, and I said, "God, if you are real and you are alive as you said, please make a way for me."

I waited, but there was no answer written in black and white to let me know. Still, slowly, God brought people and circumstances to open the door. My first miraculous blessing from God was when David Mai offered for me to stay in his boys' quarters, the extension of the house outside of the main house as I started my program, and that I could do some work around his home to help me earn money for food. In addition, he paid my tuition! He said, "Luci and I have some work for you to do, and that's how you can pay us back."

Beyond any doubt, I knew that this God I had heard about was indeed real. And I was reminded of my statement, "God, if you are real, please show me by opening the door." From that moment on, it became evident that God uses people and circumstances to show us that He is God. I had given up believing in the god that I had grown up knowing through my dad. There was no evidence of him in my world and the challenges that my family and I were going through. So, in 1986, I packed my little bag, said goodbye to Papa and Mama, and moved to ELWA to start my vocational school at LOIC in carpentry. David drove me to school every day for one month, and he picked me up after school. Then I worked around the house mowing grass, trimming hedges, scraping and painting, pruning rose bushes, and washing dishes. It was hard work, but you must do what you must do.

I went on to complete my nine-month course in carpentry. God does not come when we want Him to, but He is always on time. Indeed, our God hears our prayers, and He delights in providing for His children, whether it is food or school fees. God is faithful and good! When I completed the course, I started looking for an apprenticeship, but could not find one. So, I opted to return to school to get my high school diploma and I got admitted to Monrovia College (MC) in 1987. I left ELWA and moved to Sinkor, on 14th Street. David Mai introduced me to a gentleman by the name of Brown Thompson and asked him to host me until I could find a room. I continued to work at David Mai's house at ELWA on weekends and that is how I earned the money to pay for my tuition at Monrovia College. In 1989, I had just been promoted to the eleventh grade and was looking forward to starting my senior year of high school, when civil war broke out in our country, disrupting every institution of learning and causing many Liberians to flee.

5

Rumors and Whispers: December 24, 1989

"Words have no wings but they can fly a thousand miles"
—Korean Proverb

Life in Monrovia had kept getting better and better. My family in Firestone was happy for me that my dream was coming true. They were pleased that I was getting educated to care for our family. Papa and Mama continued to work hard at the Firestone Plantation, while I was building my little community in Monrovia—I attended a wonderful church and shared a room with six guys who became my friends and family. On the twenty-fourth of December, I visited Papa and Mama in Firestone to celebrate Christmas. I brought some food items, including some chicken and a big bag of Pusawa rice. Papa and Mama were happy that we were all in the mood for the Christmas festivities.

At six p.m., I was sitting with my Papa and our neighbor, Kerkula, listening to the news in the Kpelle language, and it was reported that fighting had occurred between government troops and some rebels in northern Liberia, in Nimba County, at the Liberia-Ivory Coast border. We didn't think much about the news report because it was considered an isolated incident far from where we lived, but people continued to discuss it in every corner of the camp.

We woke up the next morning, Christmas Day. I was excited about the big celebration because this was one of the few days of the year when we ate chicken and dressed up in our new clothes that Papa and Mama had bought and kept until this special day. Chicken was a delicacy in our house in Firestone, as on all the other days of the year we mostly ate dry bonnies (a type of dry fish commonly eaten in Liberia) with rice, cassava leaves with rice, potato leaves with rice, or with pepper soup when we were not feeling well. Firestone came alive during this time of the year with lots of cooking and entertainment.

I heard Mama yell from the kitchen outside, "Oldman! Someone is here for you." ("Oldman" was an affectionate nickname or pet name that Mama used to call me.) I went out and saw that it was one of our family friends, Mulbah SaySay, who lived in the same camp. He had heard that I was around and had come to Papa and Mama's house to greet us.

"Eddie! *Ku-maneeju?*" (meaning, "how are you?") "My Christmas is on you, ooh!"

In Liberia, we don't have Santa Claus, but rather an 'old man beggar' who dresses in a rag-like costume with a silly mask and begs for gifts, and instead of being told "Merry Christmas," or "Happy Holidays," you will hear "My Christmas is on you, ooh."

After a brief conversation with Mulbah, our neighbor Kerkula joined us. Kerkula and Mulbah talked about the previous night's radio broadcast, asking whether we had heard the news.

"Oh, yes!" Kerkula answered, "But di war 'palava' simply mean 'conflict' I don't like it."

Early Christmas morning, Mama prepared a feast with chicken gravy and rice. We ate and had a great time, and by midday, the children were all dressed up and marching around the camp showing off their new clothes. Christmas was also when Papa and Mama bought me new clothes and shoes. Later that afternoon, we got a visit from 'Old Man Beggar' with his entourage, singing and dancing. Each family in the neighborhood gave them money in exchange for their entertainment. These were fun traditions in Firestone.

After the Christmas celebration and festivities were done and the dust had settled, we faced the reality of what we had thought was a joke—the war between the government troops and the rebels.

I said goodbye to Papa and Mama and left Firestone for Monrovia to continue my schooling. Life went on in Monrovia as usual, people resumed work and continued their daily routine. For me, it meant continuing my education and looking forward to graduating from high school. However, as the months went by, the war began encroaching on Monrovia.

On February 11, 1990, the people of South Africa were celebrating Nelson Mandela's release from prison after twenty-seven years of incarceration. The news of his release echoed over the airwaves of the British Broadcasting Corporation (BBC) Radio and the streets of South Africa were filled with rejoicing, dancing, and shouting. "Free, free, free at last, free Nelson Mandela!" But in Liberia, war was raging, and people were crying and calling for help for liberation. Like South Africa, we were all men and women of the same country now divided and fighting among ourselves.

Back in school, life continued as usual for me. I was in the twelfth grade attending Monrovia College (MC) on Camp Johnson Road about three miles from the Executive Mansion. Meanwhile, the BBC continued to broadcast about the war in northeastern Liberia, telling of the brutal acts of violence against civilians by both the rebels and government troops. It was reported that in many cases, the rebels captured villages and towns with little resistance, suggesting that the people of northern Liberia, particularly Nimba County, supported the war. Nevertheless, President Doe continued to assure the nation, particularly residents of Monrovia, that there was nothing to worry about. Hence, people continued to go to work, and we went to school as usual.

We lived on Ninth Street in Sinkor, a suburb of the capital city of Monrovia, within walking distance of the Executive Mansion and downtown Monrovia. Since Ninth Street was near Tubman Boulevard, the main road into and out of the city, we often saw truckloads of government armed forces heading to the front lines in their convoys. They were dressed in their green uniforms and armed with assault rifles. It was exciting as they drove through town, so we ran to the road, cheering them on to victory as they waved and lifted their rifles in the air. While most of the trucks returned empty, the news reported that the government troops had maintained control, so we were hopeful.

In July 1990, we woke up to another newsflash: "Prince Johnson breaks away from Taylor to form another faction, the Independent National Patriotic Front of Liberia (INPFL)." In the meantime, the National Patriotic Front of Liberia (NPFL) led by Charles Taylor, continued to advance on Monrovia. Along the way, atrocities were carried out by members of the Krahn and Mandingo tribes, who were alleged to be loyal to Doe. In a BBC interview, Ellen Johnson-Sirleaf (at the time working together with Taylor) said, "Level Monrovia. We will rebuild it."

Following this interview, Monrovia suffered immense casualties and insecurity. The government soldiers took to the streets looking for rebels, setting up illegal checkpoints to extort and harass civilians. I was walking home one evening trying to beat the curfew, and I was stopped at the checkpoints, interrogated, and searched. One of the soldiers fired a warning shot in the air. I was scared for my life! My heart was pounding in my chest, blood rushing to my head. I felt confused and terrified. In my confused mind, I started begging the soldiers to release me to go before curfew got me.

Fear hovered over Monrovia. The Armed Forces of Liberia (AFL) claimed the conflict was caused by the rebel forces of Charles Taylor. The war intensified in and around Monrovia from all sides—Charles Taylor's National Patriotic Front of Liberia (NPFL) troops, the Armed Forces of Liberia (AFL) forces, and Prince Johnson's Independent National Patriotic Front of Liberia (INPFL) troops were all defending their respective positions and there continued to be even more civilian causalities from all sides. Due to the massive civilian casualties and the overwhelming humanitarian crisis, five West African heads of state met and agreed to deploy peacekeepers to Liberia. In August 1990, without any prospect for intervention by the United States or the United Nations, troops of the Economic Community of West African States Monitoring Group (ECOMOG) arrived in Monrovia to separate the warring factions and stop the bloodshed. However, this move appeared to set the stage for a confrontation between the five African nations and Charles Taylor's rebel group fighting to overthrow President Samuel K. Doe. In another BBC interview, Charles Taylor repeatedly vowed to resist foreign intervention. Charles Taylor recruited ten-year-old children, drugged them, and sent them to the battlefront. Worried about being recruited in Taylor's NPFL faction, I decided not to join with my parents for us to be together as a family since they controlled the area where my parents lived.

As a result, many were killed, and others were separated from their parents. At the same time, others died from starvation and hunger. Still others were conscripted into the children's militia. The same can be said of the government. They were also recruiting able men and youth to go into battle and repelled Taylor's forces from invading our country.

Taylor's professed goal was to end the corrupt and dictatorial rule of Samuel Doe. However, Doe's death in September 1990 did not pave the way to ending the Liberia civil war. In the final analysis, the aim of the Liberian rebellion was lost as Taylor and the other warring factions embarked on a campaign of terror against the innocent civilian population they claimed to represent. The war shifted from one of revolution to a war of genocide. Civilians suffered the most and were killed in far greater numbers than combatants. They were subjected to arbitrary arrest and detention, harassment, torture, rape, mutilation, and execution. Children were no exception! The abduction and use of children not only as fighters, but as cooks, porters and messengers, was heartbreaking. No matter their involvement, the recruitment and use of children in combat by armed forces is a grave violation of child rights.

Undoubtedly, the war was fueled by ethnic hatred and individual struggles for power while ignoring the national interest. Yet, Taylor claimed he wished to ensure peace and security in Liberia by ending the crisis. However, in accord after accord (Bamako, Lomé, Yamoussoukro II, Yamoussoukro III, Yamoussoukro IV, Geneva, and Cotonou), Taylor repeatedly refused to disarm his forces as a step toward the repatriation and the resettlement of refugees in preparation for elections. By repeatedly refusing to call on his troops to lay down their weapons as the other factions had agreed to, coupled with his poor human rights record, his image was tarnished among

Liberians whose support he'd won at the initial stage of the conflict and among regional and world leaders.

On the other hand, Prince Johnson, the other rebel leader, and President Doe said they supported the foreign military operation. As the logistical details of getting the peacekeepers into Monrovia were being arranged, there was an attack on the Nigerian and Guinean embassies. This attack on foreign diplomats caused even more anxiety and fear for civilians. The scene was chaotic to the point of frenzy—there was a massive number of people leaving Monrovia heading *toward* the fighting, and there were people fleeing *away* from the fighting, heading toward Monrovia. There was total confusion! In Monrovia, we had a government that one could not really call a government, while on the other hand, there were rebels all over the place carrying guns and ready to kill at any time. It was a situation of complete anarchy!

Heavy fighting was reported in Monrovia's eastern suburbs as Charles Taylor's troops pushed toward the fortress-like Executive Mansion of the President. Once again, a BBC newsflash: "Mr. Taylor's troops are mounting pressure to try to oust President Doe before the West African forces arrive." President Doe ordered his troops to repel the rebels from Paynesville.

I was sitting at home one afternoon when we all heard a terrible explosion. Within seconds, we heard continuous gunfire as if someone had simultaneously set off hundreds of firecrackers. We stood there looking at each other in a state of confusion.

BOOOOOOOOOOOOOM!

A second explosion was closer to us than the first one. Then we heard voices outside. People were yelling, screaming, and crying. We all panicked, ran outside, and dashed in different directions. We saw so many people on the street. One person, coming from the direction where the blast came from, told us, "Da people dey blast Jallah ooh," (a section of Monrovia near the University of Liberia.) In a state of confusion and panic, we made a decision to seek refuge at the home of one of the ELWA missionaries, Randy Wildman. We didn't believe that Randy would host us because he could be putting his life on the line, as he could be accused of harboring rebels in his house. Fortunately, to our surprise, he allowed us to stay.

Two days later, he was forcibly told by the US Embassy and the mission agency to leave the country. Full of emotion and sadness, Randy packed his briefcase, offered a prayer of protection and peace for the nation, gave us a hug, and said goodbye. That was the last time I ever saw Randy. We stayed in his house until July 31, 1990.

On the fourth day at Randy's house, we experienced something I will never forget. It has remained one of the saddest days in all of my ups and downs during the war. It was on the night of July 29th as hundreds of terrified families looking for a safer place to sleep took refuge in Saint Peter's Lutheran Church in Sinkor, just a three-minute walk from Randy's house. It was a Red Cross humanitarian shelter in a spacious building within a walled compound. It had huge Red Cross flags hanging at every corner. At dark, a group of soldiers roamed the streets, looting shops and warehouses and seeking people from Nimba County, where the rebellion had started. That night, the soldiers climbed over the wall and started killing those inside. We could hear people screaming for help and babies crying. Soldiers used machetes to hack those innocent people, including children and babies. It was estimated that six hundred people—men, women, children, and even babies—were cruelly shot or hacked to death with machetes before the order was given to stop. With this massacre creating an even greater humanitarian crisis in the city, the West African leaders could no longer delay sending peacekeepers to

Monrovia. ECOMOG troops of the Economic Community of West African States (ECOWAS) entered the conflict as "peacekeepers," but their neutrality was questioned as they appeared to aid Doe's AFL troops in repelling the NPFL.

6
Escape from the Land of Blood and Tears

"To escape means to break free from confinement or control."
—Eddie Tokpa

On July 29, 1990, the same day the St. Peter's Lutheran Church Massacre occurred, Charles Taylor bombed the ELWA radio station. He declared himself President of the Republic of Liberia and ordered President Doe's arrest. Taylor's speech aggravated the government soldiers, so they decided to pursue all perceived supporters of the rebels. I was just seventeen years old at the time.

As a result of the ELWA radio station bombing, the government soldiers targeted many of the missionary facilities in and around Monrovia, assuming they were rebel sympathizers. As an innocent law-abiding citizen, I knew, sooner or later, the soldiers would be coming over to the SIM/ELWA compound on Fourteenth Street, where I was staying with some friends (which was clearly identified with a sign) to harass and kill us. I was terrified! I kept waking up from nightmares about the rebels coming to get me. I remembered holding hands with the other two guys staying with me in the house, praying for protection for our lives during the night.

The soldiers came-to the church that night at around 11:00 p.m. They surrounded the church compound and yelled loudly, ordering the guard to open the door, but he refused. We then heard a gunshot that we thought might have been a warning shot to intimidate the security guard. It still hadn't sunk in just how vicious the soldiers were. The fact that our beloved Liberia was descending into war was unfathomable. We later discovered that the gunshot was not a warning shot, but they had killed the guard.

We then heard the soldiers shooting indiscriminately within the compound, eventually making their way over the fence. We could hear shooting within the church compound and people were crying and screaming for help as shots sprayed through the mass of people. We stood in our house less than a mile from the church, helplessly watching the scene from the window and hearing voices screaming for help.

The piercing cries of all the innocent children haunted me, as my worst fears became a reality. We saw terrified people jumping over the fence, looking for a way out. People were screaming, running everywhere, and seeking refuge from the shooters. It made me sick to my stomach, I prayed for God to make it stop, and I was sobbing.

We watched the entire scene from the window of our house, so helpless and powerless. We were unable to speak for fear we might be the next targets. A few minutes later, the church compound was silent—the soldiers had finished their massacre and left.

I could not sleep that night because I was shaking and staring into the darkness, thinking the soldiers would come to our house that night and kill us as well. Later that night, we heard the soldiers return to the compound—they were making sure that the people they had shot were dead. They continued to attack those who had come out of their hideouts. The victims cried and screamed but were met with no mercy as gunshots silenced them. We heard them shoot the many wounded to ensure their goal had been accomplished.

I sat with my two friends, J. Mac-Nixon Flomo and Nelson Cyrus, terrified. We sat silently the rest of the night, hoping God's hand would be upon us. We prayed together that God would protect us from the hands of Doe's thugs, and we also prayed for those being attacked, that God would rescue and save them. Sleepless, we waited in anticipation of daylight in order to help the injured people across the street. Dawn finally came after a seemingly endless night, and we opened our door, running to the Lutheran Church premises. As we approached, we saw people from the Red Cross and other humanitarian organizations taking out dead bodies and transporting the wounded to the hospital. We saw those who had managed to escape and hide, coming out from their hiding places. An overwhelming sense of dread came over me. At that moment, I lost hope in life and the future. Life was no longer worth living.

On July 31, 1990, at 4 p.m., two days after the Saint Peter's Lutheran Church Massacre, we heard someone knocking on our door. I yelled at the door, "Who is that?"

A man barked, "Open the door, or we will open it for you!"

At that moment, we realized it was probably the government soldiers. I opened the door and saw three soldiers at the door and another on the street near their Army jeep. One of the officers asked firmly, "Who are you, and what are you doing here?"

The other two were standing, holding their AK-47 rifles, waiting for us to respond. I quivered with fear, and tears formed in my eyes as I remembered the horrific experience at the church. Trying to remain calm, I replied, "We are students, and we are taking care of this apartment building for the missionaries."

One of the soldiers at the door, who claimed to be the commander, ordered us to get out of the building immediately without taking any belongings. Growing impatient with us, he shouted, "Get out and give me the keys!" As we stepped out of the house, he said, "The foreigners came into our country claiming to be missionaries but are spies... and we will deal with them accordingly."

My friend handed over the keys to the Army officer, and he locked the door. Meanwhile, one of the other Army officers with an AK-47 ordered us to get into their jeep. He said they were taking us to the Executive Mansion, where we would be interrogated. I looked at him in horror, as I knew the Executive Mansion was the presidential palace where executions took place.

When the commander locked the apartment door, he started questioning us further, appearing to be stalling, hoping we had some money to bribe him with. Knowing that we had nothing but food in the house, which the missionaries had left, I was losing hope with each passing minute. The commander demanded to know our identity, making us remove our shirts so he could look for markings that would indicate if we identified as rebels. It was suspected that rebels had markings on their bodies which identified them, so, whenever the government soldiers come across a group of civilians, they usually looked for that marking on men. He also made us name our tribal languages to determine which tribe we belonged to. We all said Kpelle, even though one of my friends was not from that tribe. The Kpelle tribe was seen as a neutral tribe. He was not satisfied and insisted on taking us to the Mansion. Dusk was approaching, which meant curfew would soon be enforced. We became increasingly nervous, knowing that if we remained outside a minute after six p.m., we could be accused of being rebels, which would undoubtedly lead to immediate execution. Even if they didn't execute us, but decided to release us, we would surely meet other soldiers along the way who might not have mercy on us.

As we stood on the roadside, pleading for exoneration, one of the soldiers gripped my friend's belt, pulled him into the jeep, and shouted, "Get into the car, or I will shoot you!" By this time, we knew that God's intervention was our only hope.

As I was fervently praying for God's intervention, we saw a car driving down the street. I was filled with dread as I thought it might be the Special Anti-Terrorist Unit (SATU), a specialized group of soldiers trained in Israel to provide security for the president. They were known to be the most dangerous group of soldiers throughout the war. As the car approached, it turned into the driveway opposite our apartment. It was our Lebanese neighbor and friend! He exited the car, crossed the street, and began speaking to the Army officers. He asked, "What happened?" There was a brief pause, and then one of the officers responded, "These guys are under arrest. They are Charles Taylor rebels, and we are taking them to the Mansion to answer questions." I was jolted by the term "under arrest" as it began to sink in, what was about to happen. Our Lebanese friend began to plead on our behalf and testified that he knew us well. He explained that we were the caretakers of the building and that we were not associated with the rebels in any way. He put his hand into his pocket and gave the soldiers ten dollars to let us go. The soldiers accepted the ten dollars but insisted that we should not stay in the house for our safety and protection because other Army officers on patrol in the community might still arrest us. We were so grateful to our neighbor, recognizing how fortunate we were to have someone provide assistance and speak on our behalf.

Fearing for our safety and hoping to be reunited with our families, we decided to leave. The problem was, how we could walk to our house, as it was past curfew when the soldiers left. We could only walk by ourselves if an officer accompanied us. Our neighbor also knew this, so he convinced the soldiers to take us to our rented rooms on Ninth Street (five blocks away) since they were traveling in that direction anyway. We got in their jeep and prayed they would take us where our neighbor had instructed.

As the soldier indicated, checkpoints were everywhere, especially at nearly every intersection of town. In fact, just a few blocks from the apartment, there was a checkpoint at the Saint Peter's Lutheran Church where the massacre had occurred. Checkpoints were also established along major travel routes throughout the city and at many border crossings. Informal checkpoints guarded by small groups of fighters, often child soldiers, sprung up everywhere in Liberia. These checkpoints were designed for extortion and to control any freedom of movement within the city.

There were two major checkpoints between Fourteenth Street and Ninth Street. These checkpoints had human skulls hanging on trees, so we were terrified to cross them, even with the soldiers. We stopped at the first checkpoint, and they told us that was as far as they would take us. As we began to walk to the second checkpoint, the commander ordered one of his subordinate officers to accompany us to our house. As we approached the second checkpoint, there was a loud shout, "Hey! Who are you?" I froze. Another command followed shortly, "Put your hands up and don't move!" The officer accompanying us did not utter a word and kept going toward the officer shouting at us. We remained standing with our hands up. Our accompanying officer briefly conversed with the man and then said, "Come!" as he waved us over to the other side of the checkpoint.

Relieved, we continued our journey to our house, and we finally arrived home. We knocked at the door for our landlord to open, but he was also frightened and was not willing to open the door. We then related the whole ordeal to him and explained why we had to return home from the missionary's apartment. He finally opened the door, and we went in. However, before we went to bed, we held hands together and prayed, thanking God for His protection and deliverance.

Now at home, we began wondering about our next move. Although Ninth Street was believed to be even more unsafe than the location of the missionary's apartment, it was closer to the center of town. We didn't have food or any of our belongings as we'd been forced to leave everything behind at the missionary's apartment. We were afraid to go out of our rooms, but our stomachs reminded us that we needed to brave the streets of Monrovia in order to search for food. After two days of living on only water, we decided to go to a nearby swamp, just a two or three-minute walk away. We thought we could perhaps find potato leaves and crabs to cook for lunch. Luckily for us, we caught enough for us to eat and have some kept for the following day.

After we returned from the swamp and were beginning to cook, we heard a loud blast, which shook the ground beneath us—it was close. I dropped the knife and the bowl in my hand, ran through the corridor, and went outside, where I saw a group of people standing. The blast resulted from a mortar that the rebels had launched, targeting the Mansion, but it had missed. Instead, it landed on a very densely populated civilian area a few blocks away, wounding several people.

Panic increased throughout Monrovia. The next day, the street was inundated with civilians walking toward Monrovia's main port

(Freeport of Monrovia) to escape any more attacks. We stayed behind, and Ninth Street became very deserted, eerily quiet, and lonesome. Food and water were scarce, and people were dying of starvation. We boiled potato leaves in an effort to have something in our stomachs. At night, we prayed and then decided that we would leave the area controlled by Doe's Krahn-dominated Army Forces.

On August 2, 1990, we began our journey to the Freeport of Monrovia early in the morning. At first, it was the three of us walking, and soon we were joined by several other people. The trip seemed very normal at first and no soldiers harassed us. But conditions rapidly worsened as we got to the Jallah Town checkpoint. At that checkpoint, some people had been pulled out of line because of their perceived tribal affiliations, perceived employment, or perceived family relationships—and in most cases, they were killed.

As I nervously stood at the checkpoint, one of the soldiers called a man out of the crowd and told him to remove his clothes. He stood completely naked in front of all of us. A soldier then ordered him to go across the road, and the soldier followed him to authenticate his identity. The soldier soon spotted a mark or scar on his body that he vehemently insisted indicated the man's rebel affiliation, and he was shot instantly. I became unsteady and felt like I might die at any moment. I was drenched with sweat but became quickly aware of the soldiers around me. I had to ensure that my reaction did not gain their attention, as they had made it quite clear what the result might be for me as well.

I tried to compose myself and we all made it through the checkpoint. We continued our journey, but as soon as we approached the Capitol Bypass, there was another major checkpoint. Furthermore, we were called to identify ourselves. All the women and children were told to cross the checkpoint and to continue their journey, but all the men were detained. When I approached the soldier, I started breathing hard and my heart was pounding out of my chest. I was prepared for the questions, which were always the same: "Where are you going?" "What tribe are you?" and "Where are you from?" I knew that if the soldier did not like what I said, or how I said it, or how I looked when I said it, my death was imminent. At this checkpoint, we were all asked to sit on the floor, and the soldiers walked between us to identify anyone they suspected of being a rebel or people from the Gio or Mano tribes. As we sat there, a young man was called up and the soldiers used *tabay* to make him confess that he was one of Charles Taylor's rebels. Tabay is a technique in which a rope is tied around the elbows behind the victim's back, putting extreme pressure on the ribcage and destroying all sensation in the arms. It was a common practice used by soldiers to restrain their victims and subject them to torture. We sat at that checkpoint in the sun for several hours, along with the man who was bound, until an informant came who was also an AFL soldier and said that they had received word that the INPFL (the Independent National Patriot Front of Liberia, led by Prince Johnson), was planning to attack the city. We were then quickly released from the checkpoint. I never saw the bound man again.

We continued our walk and finally reached the bridge connecting central Monrovia with Bushrod Island. Monrovia had two significant bridges: the Gabriel Johnson Tucker Bridge, which crossed the Mesurado River and connected the mainland Monrovia to Vai Town, and the Mesurado Bridge, which connected United Nations Drive and Water Street, also known as Waterside, to Bushrod Island. It was at that latter bridge that we encountered a battle. The INPFL forces were on the Bushrod Island end of the bridge, firing continuously at the government soldiers on our end of the bridge. These soldiers were then returning fire at the INPFL forces. Bullets and mortar rounds came in from the rebels, and we ran for our lives. People on the street scattered everywhere, and some took refuge in the former Europe Bank building on Crown Hill.

The bridge became a "no man's land." On our end were the AFL soldiers, and on the other end were the rebels firing rifles and launching mortars. We were far away from our house, and we were not sure if it was worth going back since it was likely to have been looted anyway. We were in a severe predicament: should we wait and see if there would be a ceasefire and, if so, cross the bridge… or should we make our way back home regardless of its condition and the dangers that might find us there? And, staying on by the bridge was becoming less of an option as we were increasingly afraid of getting hit by stray bullets, from which a number of people had died. Ultimately, we decided to stay in our makeshift hideout until there was a cessation of hostility between the AFL and INPFL soldiers.

It was already 3:00 p.m., and some people had decided not to make the trip but to remain somewhere in the city until complete calm might return so they could travel. However, we realized there would never be calmness, so we had to decide whether we wanted to go or stay. Finally, we decided to cross "no man's land"—whatever happened, let it happen. As we walked over the bridge, I was afraid, always looking behind to see what the AFL soldiers were planning to do, whether they would fire at us and blame it on the rebels. It was common practice of all the warring factions to commit an atrocity and blame it on the other group. I was faint-hearted because of the unknown and the unexpected. What if the rebels were under the bridge and might attack us? Anything was possible—one could not take anything for granted because a soldier could be laughing with you, but at the same time ordering for you to be killed. Putting one foot in front of the other, by God's grace, we crossed the bridge onto Bushrod Island and reached the first checkpoint in the rebel-held area.

Ten armed militia men aimed their AK-47s at us, and one walked toward us with his gun ready to fire. He had a red cloth tied around his head, and he asked, "Where are you all going?"

"We are going to Logan Town," one person in the group loudly answered.

Once again, the rebel soldier asked, "Is there any enemy among you?"

Once again, he answered, "No."

The militia man noted that each one of us should greet him in our respective tribal language. This was how they identified someone perceived to be Doe's Krahn soldiers. Each person greeted him in their dialect, as the other soldiers were busy searching people's bags for what they considered to be secret weapons. Eventually, each person was allowed to pass through the checkpoint. Just a few miles beyond that checkpoint, we were stopped by five rebels walking toward the checkpoint where we had just been thoroughly searched. As we approached them, one shouted, "STOP, OR I WILL FIRE!" We stopped, and once again, we were interrogated and searched. Once they were satisfied, they let us continue our journey.

We finally arrived at the Freeport, which was bustling as if there were no war in Liberia. Market people were everywhere—people moving around as though nothing were happening in the fight! People were selling water, bread, doughnuts, and every other food item you could imagine, while the people living in central Monrovia were dying of hunger! I was hungry, exhausted, and dehydrated, but could not buy anything because I did not have a penny. We kept walking until we got to Faith Healing Temple, Mother Dukuly's

Church, where internally displaced people sought refuge. When we reached the premises, the security guards at the gate told us the Church was not accepting any more displaced people because there were no accommodations. I began to panic, saying, "Lord, please help us." Curfew was approaching, and we needed to be off the street.

As we were standing at the gate with the security guard, someone came out of the church building and walked toward the gate, and the guard told us to talk to him because he was one of the people in charge of registration and management. As he came to the gate, we told him of our ordeal of escaping the AFL faction in central Monrovia to here. One older lady among us pleaded, "My son! Please help us; we don't have a place to sleep for today. Let us stay here for the night only, and we can go out tomorrow in daylight to look for a place to stay!"

We were so pitiful and weary, and we desperately needed a place to sit and rest. The man we spoke with left us standing there and went back inside to ask someone else about whether they should let us stay. Our anxiety increased the darker it got. As we waited in anticipation, we finally saw the man coming back to us. He told the security guard to open the gate and let us in. It was a huge relief that we could come inside and join other displaced people.

A lady escorted us into a hall crowded with people, malnourished children crying everywhere, sick people lying in the corners, and some were being treated by Médecins Sans Frontières (MSF) International staff. After waiting a little while in the hallway, one of the staff working with the displaced people came to speak to us. He said, "Hello, sorry for keeping you waiting. We have been discussing the issue of your accommodations here, and I am here to communicate to you our decision." He went on to say, "As you can see, we are very overcrowded here, so we are not accepting new people now. We are full! No accommodation. Furthermore, Mr. Prince Johnson came here warning us that we should get rid of all the men in here because he heard a report that there were lots of Krahn people in here. He has stopped supplying us with food because of that. We can give you temporary shelter tonight, but we will ask that you go elsewhere tomorrow. Besides, we don't have any supplies like mattresses, blankets, etc., to provide for all of you." He directed us to a church called The Little White Chapel in Logan Town, telling us that perhaps they could host us.

The following day, we started our journey to Little White Chapel. We decided not to travel along the highway for fear of coming into contact with the INPFL, so we took a shortcut, even though shortcuts could also be dangerous.

About twenty minutes into our journey, we saw a young lady with a puffed-up stomach whom INPFL had killed. We saw her body by the side of the road as we walked toward the Little White Chapel. Her heartless killers probably raped her before finally killing her because that was the day's order. As we walked further toward the church, we saw a teenage boy, who was a member of the INPFL, by the road crying with his intestines coming out through his punctured stomach. An eyewitness from the church told us that the teenage boy and his colleague had gotten into an argument, and his friend had shot him in the stomach.

We got to Little White Chapel and joined other displaced people, feeling relief that we were out of the street and had a place to stay for the time being. That evening, we ate our two loaves of bread with mayonnaise that we had bought at the Freeport of Monrovia with the bit of money we managed to escape with and went to bed. At the Little White Chapel, we would have morning devotions and midday prayer. In the mornings, there would be devotion before any activity, and people would go out to look for food. Those who stayed around attended the midday prayer. On Sunday mornings, we would all attend church services.

The major business center during the war in the INPFL-controlled area was the Freeport of Monrovia. There, transactions would take place when those brave enough to enter the warehouse at the Freeport to loot brought their goods out to sell. Every day I would join the multitude of people going to the Freeport under stray bullets, trying to find food or hoping that someone would sympathize with me to give me a jar of mayonnaise or a packet of sausages.

September 8, 1990, is a day that I will never forget. It was the day that President Doe ventured out of his besieged residence at the Executive Mansion, in an attempt to pay an official visit to the commander of ECOMOG at the Free Port of Monrovia. I woke up that morning, and as usual, joined the group walking toward the port attempting to find food or to see if someone would feel sorry for me and give me something to eat. Suddenly, we heard sirens. Surprisingly, it was the presidential convoy coming to the Freeport, which at the time was manned by Prince Johnson and his men.

As the Doe convey approached the entrance of the port, he went on top of his bulletproof jeep and waved to the crowd and his convoy drove into the Freeport compound. In the few minutes following his arrival, Prince Johnson and his troops stormed the port. Doe and his loyal ministers came under fire. Prince Johnson was known for his unpredictable behavior and no amount of logic helped when he saw Doe in his controlled area. He was the judge and the executioner in the areas that he controlled. Doe was captured and taken to the INPFL's Caldwell base on September 8, 1990, the following day, on September 9, it was then reported that Doe had been tortured and killed by the INPFL forces.

Immediately following the death of Doe, all hell broke loose in Monrovia. The AFL started destroying lives and properties. On the other hand, Charles Taylor saw the death of Doe as an opportunity for his forces to overrun Monrovia and seize power. During this period, there was serious fighting going on all fronts. The remaining AFL soldiers, who were loyal to Doe, vigorously fought to defend the Executive Mansion and their ethnic group—the Krahn. Meanwhile, Prince Johnson and his INPFL forces were also fighting to keep Taylor from seizing power.

From the onset of the war, all the warring factions had clearly stated that Doe was the one person they were coming to get. However, when Doe died, the war did not end. The carnage and the bloodshed continued. This meant more fighting and more factions developed to defend their people and communities. Lofa Defense Forces (LDF) was formed, led by Francois Massaqoui, and the Krahn and Mandingo fighters in Sierra Leone formed the United Liberation Movement of Liberia (ULIMO) led by Alhaji Kromah, in order to counter the NPFL. Within ULIMO there was a split, ULIMO-K, mostly Mandingo and led by Alhaji Kromah, and the ULIMO-J, mostly Krahn, led by Roosevelt Johnson. The Liberian Peace Council (LPC) was formed with Krahn and former AFL soldiers, led by George Boley. Finally, the Central Revolutionary Council (CRC), led by Sam Dokie and Tom Woewiyu split from the NPFL. With all of these groups formed, fighting intensified and the Cotonou Peace Agreement was ignored.

7
Weary Journeys: From Liberia to Ghana

"Oh, I am very weary
Though tears no longer flow
My eyes are tired of weeping
My heart is sick of woe"

—Anne Bronte

The five-nation West African intervention forces arrived in Monrovia on August 24, 1990, and set up heavy artillery at bridges and other strategic points in Monrovia. One of these bases was the Freeport of Monrovia. Monrovia at the time had become a patchwork quilt of rebel factions and troops loyal to President Samuel Doe. Prince Johnson's Independent National Patriotic Front of Liberia (INPFL) controlled the Freeport and most of the city center, while areas on the city's eastern fringes were under the control of Doe's forces. And these troops were under regular attack from Taylor's National Patriotic Front of Liberia (NPFL).

When it was reported that the intervention forces (which included troops from Gambia, Ghana, Guinea, Nigeria, and Sierra Leone) were arriving on that day, Charles Taylor vowed to destroy their ship, and his men attacked the Freeport. However, Prince Johnson's INPFL troops managed to repel those attacks, and the ship bringing the forces docked at the harbor. When Taylor's men failed to capture the Freeport, they advanced to the James Springs Payne Airport near the city and attacked the embassies of three of the countries contributing to the force—Ghana, Nigeria, and Guinea. They then held several thousand Ghanaian, Nigerian, and Guinean citizens captive. Meanwhile, the Ghanaian merchant ship, the M.V. Tano River, docked safely. Three days after ECOMOG troops disembarked, it was announced that the M.V. Tano River was going to be evacuating foreign nationals to Ghana.

There were two versions as to why Doe had left the Executive Mansion and gone into enemy territory. The first version has it that the Nigerian battalion of ECOMOG, which was in charge of security at the Freeport, had secured safe passage for the President, but the Ghanaian forces informed Prince Johnson about Doe's planned visit. Accordingly, INPFL forces raced to the port, disarmed and killed Doe's bodyguards, and captured him.

The other version is that Doe went to the Freeport to ask General Arnold Quainoo, who had just taken up assignment as the ECOMOG Commander, to allow Doe to take food supplies for himself and his men from the Freeport. It was then argued that General Quinanoo was the mastermind behind Doe's capture. He was said to have ordered the disarming of Doe's security guards upon their arrival at the Freeport and was accused of having informed the armed INPFL forces about Doe being in his office at the Freeport and allowing them to enter and attack the President's unarmed security guards. Regardless of the reasons, Doe was then captured and taken to the INPFL base in Caldwell, where he was tortured and killed. On September 9, 1990, Doe's naked body was displayed at the clinic on Bushrod Island.

The general impression at the time was that the removal of Doe would mark the end of the war. However, the capture and the death of Doe actually escalated the fighting and sent Monrovia into more turmoil. Meanwhile, the city had been without water and electricity for more than two months, food stocks were running low, and all regular transport links with the outside world were cut. The only access to food was the Freeport, and it was being looted and the stolen items sold.

Upon hearing the news that ECOMOG was registering foreign nationals to get on the M.V. Tano River, our small group of allies: I myself, Nelson Cyrus, Annie Cooper, J. Mac-Nixon Flomo, David Flomo, and Kopu Kennedy, decided to make our way to the Freeport, desperately hoping we would be registered as foreign nationals, and would then be able to leave Monrovia. The journey to the Freeport was a nightmare, as we met with a series of setbacks that nearly discouraged us from attempting to make the trip. However, I thought about my future and concluded that if I stayed in Liberia, my life would not account for anything under these circumstances. So, I was resolute to make my way to the Freeport, even if my colleagues were to give up. Luckily, all of us were determined to get to the Freeport despite obstacles and harassment.

The sky itself was gloomy and although it was mid-day, it appeared as if the day was just dawning. First of all, when we arrived at the first roadblock, we encountered a scene in which a young man had been shot in his leg and he was laying on the ground crying, surrounded by a multitude of bystanders, as soldiers fired in the air. We crossed that roadblock and made our way to the next roadblock, where we saw child soldiers, inflamed with their power, intimidating and frightening innocent people. At this roadblock, the soldiers separated the men from the women, as was their routine in the war, so as to identify their enemy. The soldiers allowed all the women and children to go. Soon, another soldier, who appeared to be their superior, asked to see the contents of each person's bags with his gun pointed straight at us…he said, "If you lie, we're gonna kill you." They claimed to be searching for weapons, but when they found something in the bag that they liked, they confiscated it. You could not resist them taking it; they would ask whether you wanted your life or the items. This kind of harassment was commonplace and human life appeared to have little value. I was not carrying anything valuable with me except the clothes and slippers I was wearing, and neither were my friends.

The trip to Freeport was slow and treacherous, and it seemed like it would never end. On a normal day before the war, the walk from Little White Chapel would have taken only forty-five minutes, but it took us two hours. As we left that roadblock and went on the main road to the Freeport, we saw a large group of people lining the route. Upon arrival at the Port, which was manned by ECOMOG troops, there was a large gathering of fleeing civilians standing in a queue to be registered. I asked one person in the queue, "What is going on here?" He answered, "Me and my family managed to enter here yesterday to try to get our names on the paper, but we have not been able to do that." We went to the back of the queue to get a spot. We stood in the queue from 1:30 p.m. until 4:00 p.m., but there was no indication of registration. After a long wait with nothing happening, the queue was dismantled, and people just started roaming around the premises seeking to get any information that would help them to make the decision to stay or go back home. Others were moving around networking, talking with ECOMOG soldiers, attempting to have their names on the list. I was emaciated and starving, and just leaning against an Army truck waiting to see any glimpse of registration, but there was nothing in sight.

It was approaching curfew, and the Freeport was crowded with civilians, but the soldiers were not concerned that our being there might imperil their safety or that of some in the crowd. Everyone was hungry, as hunger was a daily, almost moment to moment, experience for Liberians displaced in and around Monrovia. At that point, it was already too late to ask us to go home, because by doing so it would go against their obligation to protect the civilians' lives. So, we spent the night there with all the others, hoping that God would have mercy on us and allow us to leave.

It was indeed a huge risk and a safety hazard for civilians to be with ECOMOG soldiers, since they seemed to be an enemy of Charles Taylor. Apparently, NPFL forces coming from the Roberts International Airport engaged in fierce battles with ECOMOG forces that were manning that territory. The Nigerian and Ghanaian battalion at the Freeport received reports that the NPFL forces were planning to attack the Freeport. Upon receiving these reports, the commander in charge of the base alerted the civilian population to vacate the premises to avoid civilian casualties in the event that Charles Taylor's NPFL forces launched a mortar attack. This information caused panic, and people were weeping and pleading for the ECOMOG forces to allow them to get on the ship.

Unexpectedly, there was an upheaval—people chanting, "Let us go. We don't want to die. We are tired." The force commander tried to calm the crowds and communicate his plan of action but failed. Conversely, aware of the repercussions if Charles Taylor were to attack the Freeport, the commander ordered the entrance to the ship to be opened for us to enter. As soon as the entrance was open, it was like hell broke loose and people scrambled to get on board. I managed to get on and watched fellow Liberians tussle to enter. Two people drowned while trying to climb a rope to board the ship.

On Saturday September 29, 1990, the M.V. Tano River sailed with 7,000 displaced Liberians and those from other West African nations bound for Accra, Ghana. The journey on the ship to Accra remains the most dreadful ship ride I have ever had in my life. The ship was similar to a cargo vessel with two floors. The first floor had a large open space with a few rooms, and the second floor was just an open space with railings around that one could hold onto while sitting or standing. I was on the first floor; I got a corner, sat down, and that was my little space. The few rooms were only for the crew members, while the cargo section was for the passengers on board. The flood of people on the ship came from diverse backgrounds—rich, poor, young, old, men, women, and children—representing a cross section of Liberian society. The majority were urban dwellers who lived in and around Monrovia. Many of them were enterprising and educated young men and women, including former government officials and businessmen and women. The man sitting next to me was Lebanese, traveling with his wife and children. The trip lasted for four days, with no drinking water, food, or bathrooms to ease ourselves. It was overcrowded, unhygienic, unsanitary, and full of sick and malnourished people. It was the first time I realized that humans had strong odors. The smell on the vessel was so bad, it caused people to vomit. The wind splashed the vomit on people nearby. This lack of sanitation services caused serious health hazards on the ship.

Those who were prepared for the journey had planned ahead and brought on board little cans of water. What I had with me was one medium jar of mayonnaise and two cans of tomato paste. On the entire journey, I was licking mayonnaise and tomato paste, and sometimes exchanged mayonnaise with those who had water. On the third day at sea, people started getting motion sickness, nauseated and vomiting, because of the vessel's erratic motion on the water.

On October 3, 1990, I arrived at Tema Port in Ghana as a refugee. When we arrived, it was reported that two passengers had died of malnutrition and several people were very sick and needed immediate medical care. We had to wait on board for two hours as humanitarian workers and medical personnel took care of the emergency cases. We stayed at Tema Port for three nights, as the United Nations High Commissioner for Refugees (UNHCR) registered and vaccinated every refugee.

8

I Live in a Refugee Camp: Welcome to My World

"Refugees are individuals who flee their countries of origin because of fear of losing their lives as a result of calamities and disasters that strike their homes. The refugees seek asylum in neighboring nations with the hope of finding peace and the hope for a better future"[14]

Today, camps have become almost synonymous with the refugee experience. The essential feature of a camp is the authoritarian character of their administration; they are like 'total institutions,' places where, as in prisons or mental hospitals, everything is highly organized, where the inhabitants are depersonalized, and where people become numbers without names. Another characteristic of camps, especially those without access to land, is the persistent food shortage. There is now much evidence that refugee camps are not good for anyone. No one freely chooses to move into a refugee camp to stay. Everyone wishes to get out of there as quickly as possible. That is why almost always, more refugees live among their hosts outside camps.

One way or another, and wherever possible, these refugees become 'integrated' into the host society. The host country, in coordination with the UNHCR, provides land for refugee to make vegetable gardens and these integrated refugees are not restricted in movement, can find employment, and are better off than those living in camps. Moreover, they are not just using the resources of host institutions but are also contributing to their host's economy.

It is important to note that no one plans to become a refugee—to flee your home because your life is in danger. Yet today, there are 25.9 million refugees, more than the world has seen in nearly a century. There are many reasons a person might become a refugee. Maybe you live in a country torn apart by war and your house was bombed to rubble. Perhaps you live where you and your family are being attacked for your religious beliefs or tribal affiliation. Maybe you live in a region plagued by famine, and you are facing starvation. Or perhaps you are like me, a seventeen-year-old in 1990, and you were chased from your home by violence and placed in confinement.

I was a typical teenager living with my family in Liberia. I went to school and had many friends, anticipating graduating from high school. Suddenly, violent conflict erupted, and life became difficult and dangerous. After years of conflict, the government collapsed in 1990, and endless waves of violence continued. Suddenly, I found myself in Tema port as a refugee, standing on the shores of the Atlantic Ocean overlooking the bubbling big blue sea.

After we entered Ghana and completed our registration and vaccinations at Tema port, we were taken to Buduburam Refugee Camp, forty-four kilometers west of Accra. This camp was located in a large, remote area. Around the world, there are more than 100 refugee camps, each one different. Each one faces unique challenges, but every camp has the same primary purpose: to provide refugees with food, medicine, shelter, and protection. Life in these camps can be grim, with families crowded into hot and muggy tents. I want to share my unique camp experiences as a refugee. First and foremost, when we arrived at Buduburam camp, we had to register as a family group to receive our supplies.

Outlook of the Camp

The settlement was divided into sections using letters of the alphabet. Once we were registered and given our basic supplies, we were presented our list of "families" and assigned a tent. Other supplies included a plastic bucket, plate, spoon, cup, and mattress. My "allies" consisted of people I had connected with back in Liberia. We were friends in Liberia before, were together during the heat of the war, and we managed to escape to Ghana together. So, we had a shared experience, and grouping ourselves to form our family unit was not a problem. Our family included Nelson Cyrus as the head, since he was in his late thirties then, and his wisdom and advice were valuable as we navigated the rapids and the wave of life—first as students in Liberia, as IDPs (internally displaced persons), and then as refugees. Nelson had always been my prominent brother figure when we lived together in Monrovia with David Flomo and J. Mac-Nixon Flomo, and when we fled the war together. Nelson's fiancé and niece joined us to establish our family unit.

We were assigned the UNHCR standard-size tent with dimensions of four meters wide by six meters long. We entered, each person got a corner and put down their mattresses, and then we slept. The following day, we woke up to a grim new reality of life, a life of waiting, navigating the complicated social structure of the camp, creating a new norm, and living with our "families" crowded into our humid tents. It was a life of living in complete darkness at night and a constant shortage of food, water, and adequate bathroom facilities. Even basic supplies, like toothpaste and toothbrushes, were hard to get. It was a life where outbreaks of violence and disease were constant threats.

I remember vividly that when I first arrived at the Buduburam camp I was struck by the look of the camp. There were tall, barbed wire fences surrounding the camp and armed guards standing by the gate. At that moment, I knew how different my life was going to be. I knew I would no longer have my freedom of movement. I would no longer live in a home in a big city. I knew I would now live in a small shelter in the middle of nowhere. I knew I would no longer have access to running water as I did back in Monrovia. I knew I would have to scramble for everything, including daily meals. I was frightened both by the thought of having to live life in this manner, and of how long that might be. But early on, when we'd first arrived at Tema Port, I had made a choice to accept my new life and make the best of it.

And so, my only choice was to adapt, because for eight years I would linger in Buduburam Refugee Camp, trapped in a life of uncertainty, day in and day out, waiting for the day when peace would return to Liberia. But peace wouldn't come for a decade. Even long after I was gone from camp, the political situation in Liberia deteriorated under Taylor's regime; soon after the 2007 elections, new waves of Liberian exiles arrived in Ghana settling at Buduburam, putting a strain on the limited services and making life even more unbearable.

The addition of these newcomers also meant that there would be additional struggles to get basic necessities. It also meant that the rules and regulations governing the refugees would be tightened. I recall standing in the queue to be served a plate of rice from 4:00 p.m. until 6:00 p.m. It was a sight of unimaginable anguish—a crowd of men, women, and children stretching as far as the eye could see, scrambling and almost killing each other to get a plate of rice. Moreover, some people would jump the queue, making it impossible for people at the end of the queue to get food. This kind of pushing and shoving was only for the strong and energetic, so pregnant women, lactating mothers, the sick, the children, the injured, and the elderly were always victims of this "survival of the fittest" mentality.

Furthermore, the addition of more refugees exposed the awfulness of the camp. Facilities were not sufficient to serve the new arrivals. The conditions were terrible, with cramped makeshift tents plagued by rats. With the fresh influx, some of the new people were forced to share tents with their friends or loved ones already there. It was abject misery in the camp. The hygiene situation was appalling, and at one point there was a diarrhea and cholera outbreak in the camp due to the unsanitary conditions.

The most significant frustration about living in the camp was the daily struggle in trying to get basic necessities. For instance, getting water for baths, cooking, and drinking was a nightmare. There was no running water in the camp, and no natural fresh water sources available nearby. There were no functional boreholes or pumps in the camp. All of these obstacles left a considerable number of us without safe drinking water. As a result, many of the camp residents were vulnerable to contracting diseases. As Miller describes it, "No sound is more distressing than the plead of the homeless. Their cry expresses the pain of hunger, thirst, and disease, and denotes the fear of death, insecurity, and repression. The cry is not pretense, but a reflection of grim reality. It is an expression of tragedy occurring daily... especially in Africa where one of every two refugees resides."[5]

A few refugees were willing to walk great distances to a lagoon, but the Ghanaian government's fear of gangs and other criminal activity kept us within the confines of the camp. Water was sold from commercially operated mobile tankers as well as potable water in plastic sachets, while many refugees depended on rainfall or water from wells in the villages to survive. For our family of friends to access any of these basic necessities of life, we had to sell a portion of our rations, consisting of bulgur wheat, beans or peas, two liters of vegetable oil per household, corn soya blend, 420-gram rice sacks, cans of sardines and bar soap for laundry.

There were toilets in the camp, but access to them required that you pay money and if you didn't have any, you had to go in the bush. Many of the young girls and women fell prey to gangsters as they went to defecate. There were numerous stories of young girls and women being attacked and raped while using the bush as a toilet. Despite these atrocities, we considered the camp our home.

For many of us who did not have the connections to be repatriated to the USA or other Western countries, the camp turned into a homeland for us with no other option. The financial obligations connected to basic bodily functions were a notable source of frustration and stress for the Liberians. As refugees, the environment dictated even the most minute details of our daily lives — right down to where we could relieve ourselves. Consequently, in 1992, when the situation in the camp further deteriorated, it caused camp residents to riot, mainly over the pushing and shoving for a plate of rice as well as the unhealthy environment of the camp. It also became obvious that the best solution to this problem was to provide food rations to refugees to cook their own meals. The residents then selected a representative council comprised of two men and two women to represent the camp residents in presenting grievances to the United Nations High

Commissioner of Refugees (UNHCR), the UN Refugee Agency. The UNHCR, the camp leadership, and the camp residents' representatives met and discussed the issue and finally arrived at a conclusion that rations should be given to residents to cook their own meals.

While all this was happening in the camp, the safety inside and outside the camp was also a significant concern. The insecure environment for women, young girls, and children promoted hypervigilance among camp residents and caregivers. Many expressed fear of child abduction and rape. Parents of younger children and girls chose to keep them near the house or tents.

The menacing activities of mischievous Liberian adolescents and the hate crimes of Ghanaian outsiders were a constant source of concern. For example, the Ghanaian residents living in villages near the camp accused refugee youths of stealing from their farms. As a result, residents took matters into their own hands by beating, torturing, and abducting children. Fear for women and their children's safety caused many to remain in a state of increased tension at all times. Furthermore, fear of another war starting in the camp because of the tribal animosity caused many to live in a state of extreme anxiety and stress.

In the midst of this crisis in the camp, my body immediately went into a state of "fight or flight." There I was, my life blown apart by civil war, living in a refugee camp struggling to barely survive, and now encountering another crisis. For me, it was like getting out of the frying pan into the fire. Stress and anxiety surfaced in the core of my being. I was visibly distressed, my face was taut with worry, and my voice quivered when relating my escape from the war. I did not want to experience any more upheaval. On many occasions, I thought about leaving the camp and going back home, but every time that thought would come to my mind, I would hear of renewed fighting in Liberia, adding to my stress and anxiety. For many hours I would lay on my mattress at night with my eyes wide open recounting the overwhelming demands of the environment and my desire to leave the camp and be in a safe environment where I could resume my education.

One of the demands of the camp was the loss of autonomy for everyone, but most especially for parents. The inability of parents and caregivers to provide for and ensure the wellbeing of their children through their own efforts was stressful. The loss of autonomy for mothers and fathers promoted an expressed sense of disempowerment and helplessness. The social and economic confinement to the camp was a source of frustration for every adult, even after years of living at Buduburam. Several refugees at Buduburam received remittances from family in other parts of the world, particularly the United States and Canada, but many, including myself, were not so fortunate. We did not have any previous family connections in the US or any Western countries. Those who could not make enough to feed their children relied on the kindness of friends and neighbors or simply did without.

It is worth noting that many of the residents in the camp had held good jobs back in Liberia that made them economically well-off. Some had been small business owners, and they were independent and self-sufficient. Some worked in the government, while others were leaders in their local churches and were being paid for their service to the Church. So, making the switch from economic independence in Liberia to inconsistent subsistence living in the camp was daunting and disheartening.

As a result of this loss of autonomy, many women in the camp took on the responsibility of selling vegetable produce to help their family survive from the financial assistance they received from their family abroad. The inconsistent supply was a common theme for every family. Some women plaited or braided hair in the villages and in the local marketplaces to get money. The rest were scratching out a living through informal livelihood strategies that did not provide a predictable, consistent return. For example, some residents became domestic workers for Ghanaian families in nearby towns, providing household chores. Likewise, some worked as waste pickers, collecting recyclable materials at dumpsters and selling them to middlemen or businesses. Some people earned money by becoming street vendors selling plastic jugs of cold water, or roasted corn.

Since refugees could not get employment outside of the camp, many adopted new strategies in order to survive. For instance, children who were mature enough could sell produce or doughnuts as a means to contribute to the family's efforts to survive. One might question how we could get the capital to do business. Once we started receiving our dry rations, we could take a portion of what we had received to the nearby villages and sell them. The cash received from those sales would then be used to buy some basic necessities like bath soap, toothpaste, etc. and some of the money could also be used to invest in small businesses.

In retrospect, I sometimes ponder on how I met the demands of living in the refugee camp as a seventeen-year-old. When you are put in a difficult situation you somehow find a way to cope and adopt some strategies. For me, there were significant resources that enabled me to cope with life in the camp. First of all, a very strong coping mechanism involved the relationships that I developed with the people I came to know and referred to as family, as brothers and sisters, and with whom I shared accommodations. We cried together on many occasions as we shared common experiences and talked about our family members we were separated from. We also laughed together as we reminisced about licking mayonnaise and tomato paste back in Liberia and on the ship. I adopted livelihood strategies including becoming a shoeshine boy and selling plastic bottles of water as a subsistence activity, trying to survive with limited resources in a limited environment. I also sold kerosene to camp residents which they used in their lanterns to provide light.

Additionally, the psychosocial support of the Church was paramount in helping me cope with life in the camp. Christianity had previously been a major source of my development. My faith in God was a powerful source of psychosocial and spiritual support, as well as a means for active coping. Spiritual support of other Christian believers reinforced a positive sense of identity and bolstered hope and allowed me to keep trusting for a better day to come. On many occasions, I joined with other Christians in the camp to pray as we encouraged and supported each other. I lived in a tent with six people, and we all believed that God had helped us in the past, He was helping us in our present circumstances, and He would help us in the future. We prayed together every night before we slept.

Surely, God provided for each one of us mysteriously. He would eventually provide me with a scholarship through a "Good Samaritan" to complete my high school education while still living in the refugee camp. He would do the same for each of my friends. A mission agency in Ghana called Sudan Interior Mission (SIM), prior to changing its name to Serving in Mission (SIM), would give Nelson Cyrus a full scholarship to attend Maranatha Bible College in Accra, Ghana. J. Mac-Nixon Flomo would go to school in Nigeria. My cousin, David Flomo, would go to Daystar University in Nairobi, Kenya, and later would earn his master's degree in social work at the George Washington School of Social Work in the United States.

Our firm belief in a loving God who was watching over us and protecting us was uplifting amid a devastating existence in the camp. As a teenager, I lived on the margins of society, unwelcome in Ghana, and sometimes associated with a group of Liberian gangsters going around Accra robbing people of their money. Our day-to-day lives were characterized by inconsistent subsistence and inaccessibility to primary resources. As Agiers writes, "Each displaced person, each refugee, carries within them the experience of being undesirable and placeless."[6] As refugees in Ghana, we felt unwanted by the local community. I must admit that our faith in God as refugees spoke a different message than those resonating within our daily experience in the camp. We were accepted by God and welcomed. We were not lost to Him but rather very near. In a situation characterized by scarcity and inconsistency, God was always listening and ready to provide for our needs. His provision for my friends and me, no matter our losses or difficulties, was always an empowering source of meaning and purpose for us.

It is imperative to note that church involvement also contributed to a positive identity by creating opportunities to obtain a social status within the community. I was among the body of believers that founded the Christian Fellowship, the Liberian Interdenominational Assembly (LIDA), and I served as an usher in the church. Interacting with other Christians gave me a feeling of worth in the community. As refugees, isolated from mainstream economic opportunities and socially marginalized, we were the least significant in Ghana. Most of us held no official job, and our days were filled with the essential tasks of survival, but leadership positions in the church and participation on committees and choirs provided opportunities for recognition and a sense of importance. The church also functioned as a gathering place for social and emotional support. I always felt happy at church; it was a place to meet friends and be encouraged. It provided a means of active coping, and alleviated anxiety and stress, at least temporarily.

I can't talk about the refugee camp without mentioning education. There was no school the first two years after we arrived in the center. Most of the children and youth in the refugee camp were out of school due to hardship and the inability of their parents or guardians to send them to school in Ghana.

Since my experience, there has been significant progress in dealing with disaster and conflict areas around the world, from Uganda, to Chad, Kenya, Ethiopia, and others. This includes giving refugees access to schools, making school timetables more flexible, offering exceptional help to children to catch up on missed school years or to learn new languages, for training camp residents to become teachers, providing more educational materials, and helping children adjust to the challenges of life as a refugee. The rise also reflects a commitment by the Ghanaian government to include refugee children and youth in their national education systems—an essential, fundamental strategy for boosting enrollment.

Providing refugee children with educational opportunities, proper curriculum, and school certification is the pathway to progressing to secondary or higher education, with which someone like me could have finished my high school education.

Our situation in Ghana made it challenging for refugee parents who could not afford to send their children to Ghanaian schools. Parents only had the option to seek sponsorship from Non-Governmental Organizations (NGOs) or allow their children to stay at "home." But during my time there I saw a change.

In the third year of being in the camp, UNHCR established a primary school, though they initially refused support for high school or university students. These small gains were thanks to impressive efforts by the host government, donors, UNHCR, and partner organizations to get more refugee children into the classroom.

By the grace of God, in 1993, I was given the opportunity to complete my high school at Ghana National College in Cape Coast. At the time, the cost of Senior High School was Ghc (Ghanian Cedi) 2000, which was approximately $550 for an academic year. I would not have been able to complete my high school education if God had not sent a good Samaritan to help me along the way. Many refugee youths like myself could not afford this high cost of tuition. As a result, many school dropouts were found roaming around the camp without a sense of purpose. Eventually, they became addicted to social activities like playing soccer (which I did), weightlifting, playing the game of Ludo, going to nightclubs and other entertainment centers, and doing drugs. And those who wished to become breadwinners for their families sometimes chose illicit paths such as child labor, prostitution, and crime. Wayward children as young as thirteen could be seen pushing wheelbarrows as a commercial transport to earn money while others, especially girls, washed clothes for a living.

Living in the camp opened my eyes to seeing education as an investment because it put people on the path towards empowerment. From his work with Liberian refugees in the Ivory Coast, Utas (2004) observed that "Liberians' intense urge to have their children educated stemmed from two contextual sources. First, they had lost all other wealth acquired through their lifetimes, and education was the one resource that could not be looted. Second, especially for those who came from urban areas, education increased their ability to obtain higher quality jobs."[7] My prayers were always that God would help me acquire an education so that when I returned to post-war Liberia

I could be a productive citizen and make a contribution to the development of Liberia.

As mentioned previously, I would like to reiterate that life as a refugee is dehumanizing, and refugees are often branded as threats, turned back at borders, left to perish at sea, or detained indefinitely in horrific conditions and denied their humanness. In the camp, they mostly changed your name into a number—they called you A1 or A2. "A1" or "A2" is the number on your tent supplied where you live. Our nickname for the camp was "Jungle," depicting that humans could not live in such conditions and that the settlement was built in a remote area. Life in the camp is a constant struggle for survival. No movie, no picture, no book can show the extent of the tragedy and the complexity of life in a refugee camp. I can only sum it up: "You need to see it and live it!"

9
An Unexpected Opportunity and God's Rescue

"In the middle of difficulty lies opportunity."
—Albert Einstein

It was an ordinary day, as usual, in the refugee camp. I woke up, brushed my teeth, and put on my clothes, waiting for the sound of the bell to go and line up for my cup of porridge and a slice of bread. I took my porridge and bread to my tent and ate, contemplating what to do. A friend walked by and asked if I wanted to take a walk to the nearby village. But of course we had to follow the necessary protocol that governed exiting the camp. First, we had to go to the camp commandant to obtain a written slip of paper authorizing the police to allow us passage. We got the necessary authorization paper and brought it to the police.

We signed in the police record book and walked three miles into a Ghanaian village, not for anything in particular, but just to escape the camp environment for a short while. When we returned from our walk, a friend approached me and said, "Eddie, you need to go to the commandant's office. We heard your name on the loudspeaker. They want to see you. They have a message for you." I was terrified and distraught. In most instances, you're summoned to the commandant's office because someone lodged a complaint against you or you committed an offense that needed to be addressed.

I had so many thoughts running through my mind: why would they want to see me? I wondered. I didn't know anyone in Ghana who could come to visit me. Had they traced my family to neighboring countries? Perhaps that's why they were calling to tell me, or did I break any camp rules?

Nevertheless, I composed myself and walked to the commandant's office. When I arrived at the office, I saw a Caucasian man sitting down. The commandant asked, "Are you, Eddie?"

"Yes, I am Eddie" I responded.

He went on, "Do you know this man?" pointing toward the gentleman.

I replied that his face looked familiar. At that point, the Caucasian man introduced himself. "I am Mark Bruner. I work with SIM." He went on to say, "We received this letter from David Mai, and he wanted us to come and look for you and other friends."

As I looked at the letter from my old missionary friend who'd helped me so much with my education, I smiled and wiped away tears as I hugged Mark. "Thank you, Lord," I repeatedly prayed as I walked with Mark to see my other friends. I was reminded again of God's intervention for me in Liberia, and I had once again seen that God is "Jehovah Jireh," our Provider. Nothing is impossible with Him. As I was on the verge of giving up, God became more aware of my ugly situation at the camp, and He began to orchestrate a way to get me out of the camp somehow.

I had a lengthy conversation with Mark about my escape from Liberia, life in the camp, and the challenges I faced. It was the most fantastic moment of my life, and I will never forget it. Even now, as I remember that afternoon, it brings me to tears. Just as God opened the eyes of a blind man to bring glory to Himself, God was opening my eyes. For the first time, I could see Him, sense His presence, and understand that He was real. God comes through many sources, even just a listening friend. Mark Bruner was indeed who God had sent at the right time to comfort me. God uses us to comfort one another with the comfort we have received from Him. It is both a privilege and a responsibility. As we tell others of God's faithfulness amid trials, it reminds us that God will never forsake us. Though we may walk through the valley of the shadow of death, we will never walk alone.

Mark Bruner asked if I wanted to write a letter to David Mai and said he would ensure that the letter got to David. So, I wrote a letter about being in Ghana and living in the refugee camp. I expressed my gratitude to him for reaching out to me.

Sometime later, Mark again visited the camp, but this time he had a letter from David Mai addressed to me. When I received the letter, I was overwhelmed and burst into tears. It was like a dream! I decided to make contact with David.

At that time, email was not very popular, and communication overseas was mainly through snail mail. I did not have his email address or his mailing address until I received his letter from Mark. Until then, I didn't know how I could contact him directly. So, I wrote back to David again and sent it via Mark Bruner. In my second letter to David, I was very candid and requested financial assistance to complete high school. And his response to my letter was positive. The following year, in September 1993, I started my new adventure at a government boarding school in Cape Coast called Ghana National College (GNC) with my cousin David Flomo, about a three-hour drive from the refugee camp in southern Ghana! "I am not going to miss this opportunity," I said to myself. I was going to grab it with my two hands. As Albert Einstein said, "In the middle of difficulty lies opportunity." Einstein's quotes urge us to change our perspective on challenges. Instead of focusing on the negative aspects of difficult situations, we can choose to see the potential benefits and opportunities for growth and success that they present to us. Flomo was the epitome of choosing not to focus on the negative aspects of difficult situations. He was upbeat, joyful, and, above all, very studious and was a tremendous source of encouragement and support for me during our time in exile and in National College.

This was *my* opportunity! All during my stay in the camp, I had been dreaming and scheming for this opportunity, and it was now time to pay the price of commitment and take hold of my opportunity before it slipped through my fingers. However, commencing an academic journey in a foreign land as a refugee could be very daunting, and in my case, it was convoluted with many additional issues. First, I did not have transcripts from my former school, so it was hard for the admissions office to determine where they needed to place me in the Ghanaian educational system. To minimize the decision-making process, I requested to take an entrance exam that could help them determine what grade they needed to place me in. Finally, they agreed that I could take the entrance exams in two subjects: English and mathematics.

I passed the entrance exams, but then there was another problem: the Ghanaian educational system would not allow me to spend only one academic year, even though I was in my final year of high school before the war. Ghana operates on a '6-3-4-4' system. That is, primary education is six years, junior secondary/high school is three years, senior secondary/senior high School is four years, and university is four years. Completing any of these levels and moving to the next is competitive, requiring students to write an intense final examination. Furthermore, the curriculum is designed to prepare the student for the final exam at the secondary/high school level. This educational system and the curriculum are all geared toward this one final examination. Therefore, I had to spend four full years in high school in order to receive the necessary preparation for this final exam as required by the examination council.

Ghana has a wide range of ethnic groups, each with its distinct language, and students tend to speak their ethnic language to members of their ethnic group. But Ghana's official language is English, inherited from the British colonial era. Therefore, English is used in education, government, and business and is spoken fluently by many Ghanaians. Twi and the Fante are Ghana's two most widely spoken indigenous languages, which I tried to learn and was not very fluent. That made it difficult for me to interact, but I quickly figured out how to navigate my new social world with the few phrases and ethnic language I could speak.

I learned to ask many questions in order to understand what was being communicated in the required language. I was always seeking information, trying to understand my new culture. I also observed that nearly all the students had nicer clothes than me — something I quickly had to accept and adjust to. There were only two non-Ghanaian students in the school of 556 students. So, I developed a pretty nice core group of friends who were some of the nicest in the school, who just liked me for me, and were interested in hearing my story.

Two of those kids were Jewel Ashie and Samuel Abbey, who became our school friends and roommates. I met Jewel and Abbey in the dormitory corridor when I was getting acclimated to my new surroundings. They were also relatively new to the school, so we bonded over being new students. We also connected over different cultures. I was a refugee from Liberia, and they were both Ghanaian. I was interested in learning about their cultures and stories; likewise, they were interested in hearing my story and learning about the war. We all were in the same class, and we studied together. One day, one of the other students tried to bully Jewel, and I stood up for him. From then on, he started referring to me as his "school father." We often hung out, and I went home with him to visit his family. Whenever his parents came for a school visitation, they always brought a little gift for me.

My outgoing nature, along with my ability to be adaptable, helped me settle into that new, unfamiliar environment quickly. It is essential to say that only a few people at Ghana National College became my friends because I often put people off by my thick Liberian accent. Some did not like Flomo and me with our upbeat and big smiles. Coming from war, they expected us to be sad and worried about life, especially since we did not know the whereabouts of our parents. Of course, we were nervous and concerned about the wellbeing of our families, but worry could not help to make our lives or our situation any better. Many of the students saw us as social rivals, but we were determined to make the best of the opportunity. However, the more I got to know the well-off and not-so-well-off kids, the more I grasped that people often had similar struggles. On the surface, we may appear different, but we are the same at our core. Kids from wealthy families were struggling and depressed about life and academic work as well. Refugees have the unique ability to overcome their environments when given the tools and opportunity to do so.

On a side note—thank God for Facebook! Jewel, Samuel, and I recently reconnected, and we communicate regularly. Jewel lives and works in the United Kingdom and Samuel Abbey lives and works in Ghana.

10
Higher Education

"Education is the most powerful weapon which you can use to change the world."

—Nelson Mandela

Toward the end of my studies at Ghana National College, I was confronted with another difficulty. Everyone talked about what they would do at home with their parents and siblings when they returned. I had no home or family to go back to. My home was the refugee camp, and my family was Flomo and my friends who'd escaped with me to the camp. Seeing the other students preparing to leave made me sad and homesick. I not only had no home to go to, but I had no family either. I did not know the whereabouts of my parents. I was not living with them at the time of the war. Many years later, I came to learn that my parents had escaped to Guinea and stayed in a refugee camp, and there they died. I was told that they got sick and did not have medical treatment and eventually passed away.

Unlike other schools, our school did not have a guidance counselor to help students with decision making. I graduated, wondering what my next course of action should be. I was at a crossroads, but my options were minimal. One option was going back to the refugee camp, or I could go back to Liberia to look for my family. With these limited choices, I chose the former.

My hopes and ambitions were to continue with my studies. I had thought I was starting a new life by leaving the camp for school. Instead, I saw my life moving in a direction that I didn't like; I disliked the idea of going back to the camp to a life of stress and trauma. However, I did not have many options or abundant choices. Therefore, I did not have the luxury of time to decide what I should do next. One gift life does not give us is an abundance of time, so I quickly decided to go back to the camp to face the challenge, not in anger, fear, or defeat, but with more vitality, hope, determination, and a longing for education and a brighter future, than when I was there before.

At the end of the school year, I said goodbye to my Ghanaian brothers and sisters who had become part of my life, picked up my few belongings, and I was on my way to the camp. I was glad I had acquired my high school diploma, a stepping-stone for additional education, but I was very sad that I was not going to further my education. Instead, I was going back to the refugee camp and praying I would not wander and waste my life.

When I arrived at the camp, the road of life there was bumpy, but I decided to get a firm grip on the steering wheel and set goals and plans that would guide me. I knew that becoming negative would only make the experience more painful. On my return to the camp, I knew that the education I had received at GNC out of the textbooks was but a small part of the life lessons I would learn. One of the things that impressed itself upon me intensely during my return was the unselfishness of fellow Liberians and their families in accepting new incoming refugees into their family units as dependents. They took in newcomers who were in desperate need of shelter, food, and a safe space for their children. The generosity of Liberians in the camp was admirable; though they did not have enough and heavily relied on the UN for their survival, they were willing to share with others what they had.

During my time at school, most of my friends had left the camp. Most of them had been resettled in the United States or Canada, while a few were in Accra pursuing their studies. While networking and connecting with some of those friends in Accra, I heard about Ghana Christian College and Seminary, where many Liberians were studying. I decided to visit the campus to see some of my colleagues, but during my visit, I also took the opportunity to inquire about admission. I had heard it said that one needs an education to get anywhere in life, so I had always had that in the back of my mind.

Stephanie Owen and Isabelle Sawhill claim that "Additional education improves overall well-being by affecting things like job satisfaction, health, marriage, parenting, trust, and social interaction." (Owen and Sawhill, 2010).[8] Ultimately, Owen and Sawhill are saying that the outcome of obtaining an education will have a significant impact on your overall self and future. So, my pursuit of higher education stems from that background.

On that visit to Ghana Christian College and Seminary, I expressed my interest and shared my needs and situation with the principal. He had compassion for me and offered me a scholarship for three years. After our conversations, the principal prayed for me and the situation in my country. This act of generosity reminded me of the many kindnesses of others in my life and restored within me the belief that people are intrinsically good.

As I sat in the principal's office, I said to myself, "I will have to mirror this act of kindness, compassion, and generosity shown to me by so many people." I wouldn't be who I am today without them. Their acts of love, compassion, and generosity have allowed me to become a strong person who is determined to better his life. My experiences of living at Firestone Plantation and seeing my parents' struggles, seeing exploitation at the highest level, being a refugee, and seeing my friends succeed and leave the camp, all encouraged me to want to acquire an education that would give me a foundation to turn my life around.

After I graduated from Ghana Christian College and Seminary in 1997, the war in my country was at its peak. Of course, it meant I couldn't return home even if I had wanted to. Hence, I decided to seek further study. Toward the end of 1997, I started looking for universities around West Africa and East Africa, particularly Nigeria, Ghana, and Kenya. I applied to universities in these three countries with the hope and trust that God would provide the resources as He had done in the past. Of the three universities I investigated, Daystar University in Nairobi, Kenya, responded to my admission request and sent me a prospectus and application package. I went through the material, and I decided this was the school I wanted to attend. With enthusiasm, I began the application process. I submitted all of the requirements on paper, but the one thing lacking was the actual assurance of sponsorship. Although I had indicated and assured the university that I had the money to cover my four years of study at Daystar in practice, I had no guarantee or assurance from any individual for that sponsorship.

Meanwhile, as my application was in progress, I embarked on a journey to secure a scholarship. I needed to figure out where and how to begin sourcing funding. So, I wrote a letter to David Mai, explained the situation, and forthrightly asked if he could raise money for me for my first year of college. One month passed, and I had not heard from him, and I was beginning to worry, wondering if I had upset him or if I was becoming a burden to him and he had decided to withdraw. That period of silence was one of the scariest times in my life. I could not fathom losing him in my life during that stage. He was a father, a counselor, and a teacher in my life. But, it turns out, in that moment of silence, David was busy sharing my story with his circle of friends and colleagues to raise money for my schooling.

Finally, I heard from David. "I am sorry for the delay in getting back to you! We managed to find money to get you started with your school. I can't promise full support, but we will be able to help as God leads us. In the meantime, we'll continue to share your story with our friends here to see if they can help." When I read this, I was exhilarated because that was all I needed to know. I did not grow up being a perfectionist, needing to know every detail and having everything planned out, but rather to live and take one day at a time. I learned this concept at a young age, and living in the refugee camp reinforced the mentality of living one day at a time. I lived each day in the camp as if it were my first and last. If it was time for soccer, weight training, standing in a queue to get a plate of rice, or banku, red-red, and kenkey (a type of local Ghanaian cuisine), which I participated in with all my might.

Banku is made with ground corn and cassava, molded in a thick, doughy ball, and commonly eaten with grilled tilapia or soups and stews. The fermentation of the flour gives them a slightly sour taste that needs balancing with a rich spice sauce and some hot peppers. On the other hand, kenkey is often compared to an extreme version of sourdough bread. Unlike sourdough bread, kenkey is made by shaping corn and cassava ball-like dough, wrapping it in banana leaves, and leaving it somewhere warm for a few days to ferment. It is usually eaten with a marinated grill, fried fish, or stew. The stew is made from a mixture of tomatoes, ginger, onion, and peppers blended in a food processor, then cooked and seasoned with salt and bouillon powder to taste. Finally, red-red is a simple Ghanaian stew made with palm oil, beans, tomatoes, and chicken stock, flavored with chili and ginger, and served with fried plantain. It is one of the most accessible and best loved of Ghana's dishes and is the starting point for most new visitors.

Not worrying about tomorrow and living in the now was the most effective and quickest way of overcoming my stress and anxiety. Getting the opportunity to attend Daystar and knowing that my first-year's tuition was taken care of was all that mattered. On January 5, 1998, I arrived at the Nairobi airport on Ethiopian Airlines during the El Nino weather phenomenon. I was stranded at the airport for several hours because rainfall had destroyed the bridge linking the Daystar Athi River campus and Nairobi. The shuttle finally arrived, and I was taken to Daystar, Athi River campus.

The alarm went off at 6:00 a.m. I got up from bed and took a cold shower. As I brushed my teeth and combed my hair, I mentally noted the tasks of the day ahead: go to the dining room and have breakfast, and then proceed to the Admissions Office. I was very nervous and afraid! One might think that I should have been excited, but I was scared. I don't know why I was worried, perhaps because the environment was new, and being at a prominent university was also a factor. I walked into the dining room, grasped my plate, and took my two slices of bread, two mandazis (a form of sweet fried bread similar to doughnuts), and a cup of tea. I sat at an open table all by myself, but shortly, as luck could have it, one other student walked straight to my table, greeted me, and asked if he could sit with me. "Of course," I said. We started having a conversation, and it turned out he was a newcomer like me. His name was Powon Kapello. Coincidentally, we shared a room in the dormitory and were in the same department.

Without trying to sound dramatic, my attendance at Daystar changed the trajectory of my life. I met friends like Powon, with whom I could explore new ideas and theories in our studies. I learned from him that each person you meet is complete with their thoughts, opinions, and beliefs. I met Kenneth Dachi, who taught me that the inevitable twists and turns of our lives down the long and winding road that represents our journey are made sweeter and more meaningful by the sharing and caring of a good friend. Ken and I supported each other in one of the difficult moments in our lives after graduation. Both of us were at a crossroads in our lives. He had just fallen out with his business partner and was looking for a job and a place to live, and I was thinking about going to Liberia and raising money for airfare. So, Ken moved in with me, and we shared life, went to Church together, cooked meals together, and prayed for one another for God's provision in our lives during that transition period. He would buy groceries, laundry detergent, and cook when he had money. I would also do the same.

Alex Jami introduced me to Nairobi Chapel (a place I could go to be nourished spiritually), and he laughed with me on many occasions as we served together in the Study Abroad office. These experiences, among many others, helped shape the person I became.

I registered and started my classes. I ended my first year successfully, but during the summer after my first year I received a heartbreaking letter from David Mai. He explained he would not be able to provide financial support for me because he was going through a divorce and was dealing with that crisis. I was so crushed and disillusioned. I could not grasp the thought of going back to the refugee camp. I walked to Lukenya Hill, a prominent inselberg, an isolated rock hill in the plains east of Nairobi near the University, to pray and ask God for direction. As I sat on top of that rock, I thought of so many examples of people in the Bible who faced seemingly impossible situations. When the Israelites saw Pharaoh's soldiers in the distance charging toward them, it appeared as though they were trapped with no apparent way out. Terrified, the people cried out to Moses in despair. There seemed to be no hope for them at all. But Moses trusted God during this impossible time.

Moses didn't get upset, give up, or give in to desperation. Instead, Moses steered the people's attention to God and calmly gave a solution as he said, "Do not be afraid. Stand firm. And you will see the deliverance of the Lord. The Lord will fight for you while you keep silent." (Exodus 14: 13-14.) God then told Moses to tell the people of Israel to "go forward." Moses lifted his staff, stretched his hand over the sea, and divided it. God intervened, for sometimes He prefers to work in a situation that some deem impossible. He dramatically caused a strong wind to blow. The waters parted and the people safely walked on the sea floor, on dry ground, to the other side.

Similar to the Israelites, we can also be put into a temporary yet challenging place or a seemingly impossible circumstance. Yet what looked like a mess for the Israelites, God turned into a miracle. As I reflected on this powerful story of God's intervention in the life of the Israelites, it provided some level of consolation for me and to believe that He loves me as His own and would take care of me and intervene in my situation.

I came down the hill feeling like a heavy weight had dropped from my shoulders. As the semester began, I met with Ms. Marsha Navamanie, the special assistant to the vice chancellor and the Daystar US Scholarship coordinator, to discuss my predicament. As I started sharing my story, she immediately told me she had already received communication regarding my situation. "It is a difficult situation," she said. "You will have to take a semester off as we work out how to get you on the Daystar US scholarship." She said, "You will also have to vacate the dormitory and stay in Hostel B." Just before I left Marsha's office, she prayed with me and told me to apply for Daystar

US sponsorship, but there was a requirement. "You must have a GPA of 3.0 and be enrolled in the work-study program." I immediately applied for the scholarship and awaited the committee selection.

At this point, I felt God was already intervening in my situation. The next day, I packed my stuff and moved to Hostel B, a private rented house for students who could not afford to live in the dormitory. I took the semester off, but interestingly, nobody knew that I had taken a semester off, except my roommates, because I participated in every activity except for attending class, and seeing that no one asked, life went on. The response from Marsha taught me that we don't meet people by accident. Every person you meet will play a role in your life, big or small, and that has been the story of my life. Some will help you grow, some will inspire you to do better. At the same time, you are also playing a role in their lives.

At the end of my semester off and the beginning of September 1999, I saw my name on the noticeboard among those selected for the scholarship. My spirits brightened, and joy took hold of me. I was determined to take advantage of the opportunity presented to me. I recommenced my studies, and it was finally time in 2002 for me to walk across the stage at graduation with a degree to show my efforts in pursuing higher education. It was a hallmark moment filled with smiling, inspirational speeches, and group pictures to forever capture that feeling of accomplishment. However, what often gets overlooked in the afterglow is the question that lurks in the mind of most every recent graduate: What next? That was the question for me. The war was raging in Liberia, so I could not go there. I decided to look for an internship to buy time as I weighed my options of going to Liberia or going back to Ghana in the refugee camp.

I applied for a pastoral internship at Nairobi Chapel in 2003. My primary intention was to use the position to learn about ministry and church structure. I owe a great deal of gratitude to Nairobi Chapel and wish to thank, the leadership of Nairobi Chapel for allowing me to serve and learn as an intern. By allowing me to serve in this manner, I could sit in Church service planning meetings and observe firsthand how to deliberately and methodically serve the people in the church. I also spent quality time with Pastor Dr. Omar, Heather Webb, and Bob Kikuyu in weekly one-on-one meetings where I could learn from them and ask related questions. In those meetings, I was also provided with the opportunity to refine particular skills that would serve both me and those people I had yet to meet. I was also able to improve my preaching skills, as I was granted the opportunity to serve in the Prison Ministry and a church in Buruburu in the Eastlands part of Nairobi. I will forever be grateful for what they did for me.

Nairobi Chapel gave me the opportunity to attend Theological School in Nairobi at Nairobi Evangelical Graduate School of Theology (NEGST) to deepen my pastoral care training. In 2005 I received my Master of Arts degree in Missions from NEGST.

Sadly, the unimaginable happened when I later moved to the United States: my international college degree was not validated because the school was foreign to educational institutions. I would not be offered a job! Furthermore, my transcripts could not be accepted to enroll in a university. I was asked first to have my transcripts evaluated by a professional evaluation service, to see which of my credits would transfer as per US requirements. I was also made to write an essay stating that I was mature enough to pursue a master's degree at US institutions. Because I was discriminated against based on my educational attainment, I decided to comply, have my transcripts evaluated, write my essays, and eventually enroll in a university for a second master's degree. After going through these processes, I was finally admitted to Eastern University in 2014 and graduated in 2016 with a master's degree in international development.

Eddie's brother tapping a rubber tree on the Firestone Rubber Plantation.
(Personal photo)

David Mai, Eddie's Missionary friend from ELWA
(personal photo)

Refugee Camp (personal photo)

Mark Bruner's visit to Buduburam Refugee camp to deliver letter from David Mai. Left to Right: J. Mac-Nixon Flomo, David Flomo, Mark Bruner, and Eddie (Credit: J. Mac-Nixon Flomo)

Eddie in the field in Buduburam Refugee Camp (Credit: Linda Watt)

Eddie with a group of friends in Buduburam Refugee Camp, Ghana, West Africa
(Credit: Eric Massaley)

Ghana National College, the High School Eddie attended in Cape Coast, Ghana (person photo)

U.S. Citizenship (Credit: Gary Baughman)

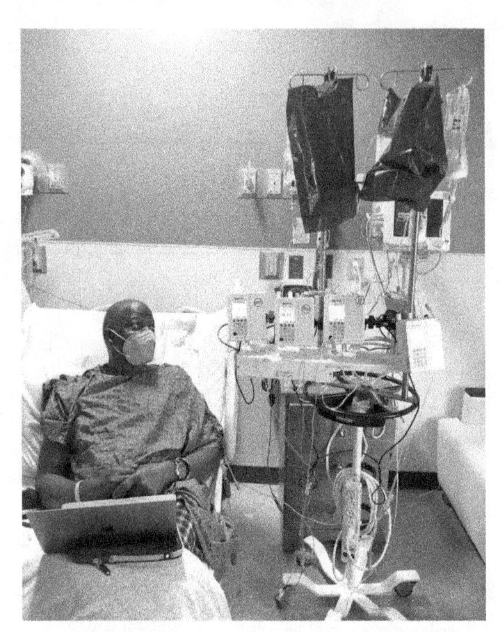

Eddie at Presbyterian St. Luke's Medical Center for chemotherapy
(Credit: Gary Baughman)

Eddie's Family, from left to right: Lisa, Zeke and Eddie
(Credit: Gary Baughman)

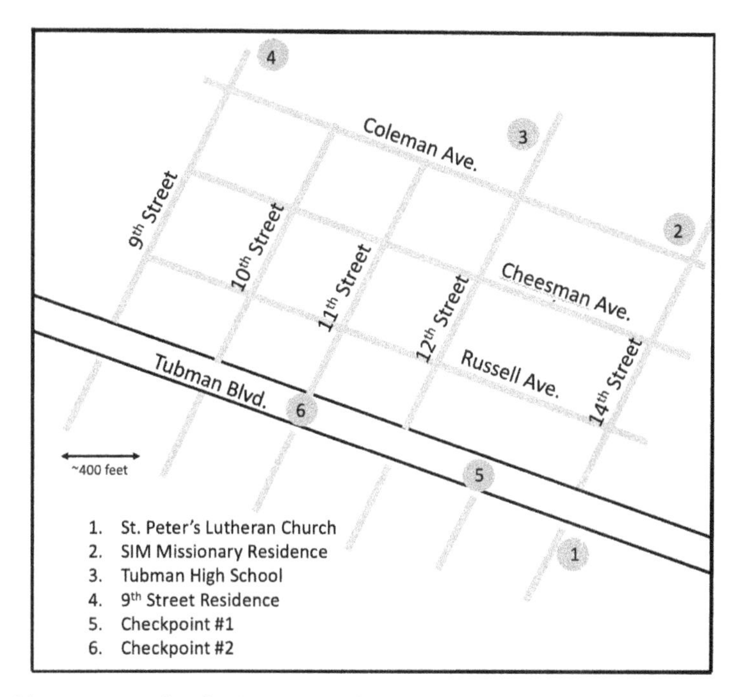

Key sites in the Sinkor area of Monrovia before Eddie's escape

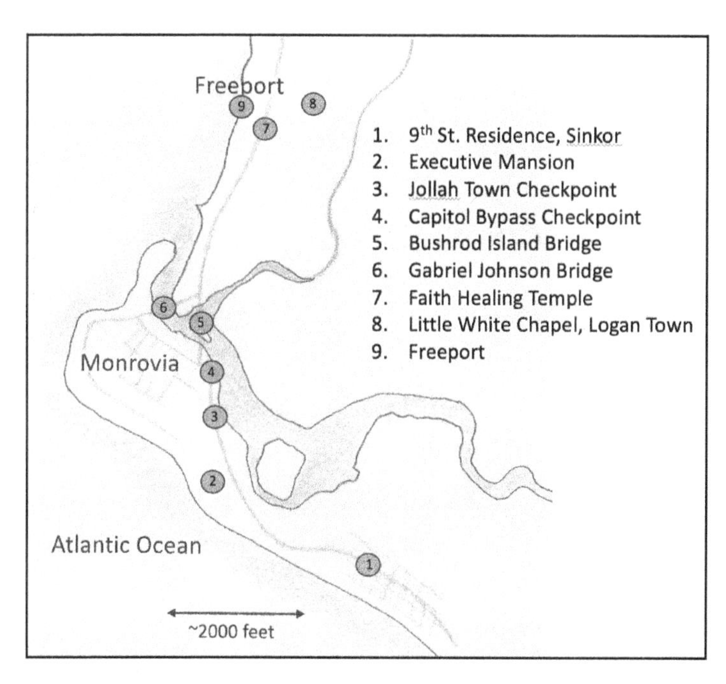

Key points during the escape to Freeport

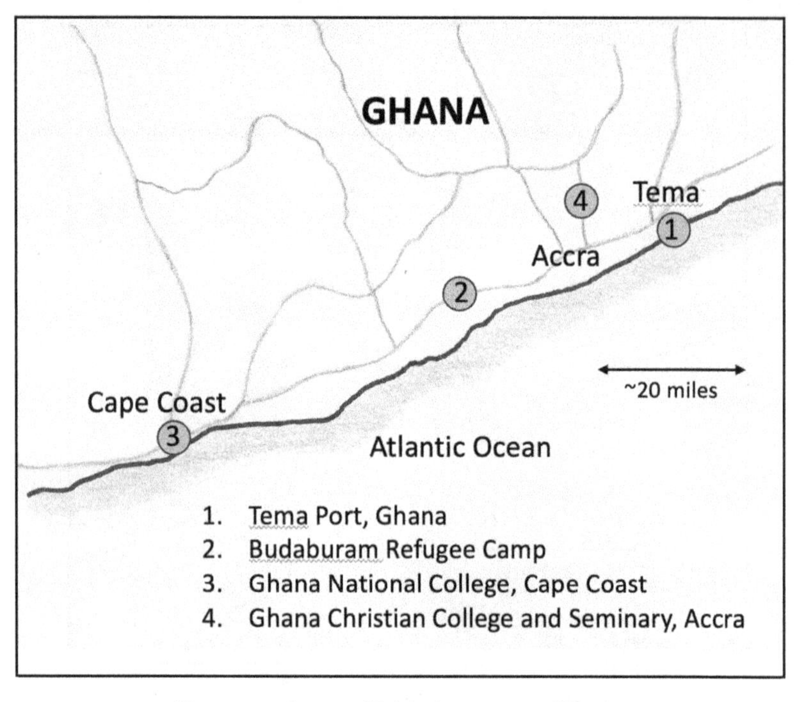

Key sites during Eddie's time in Ghana

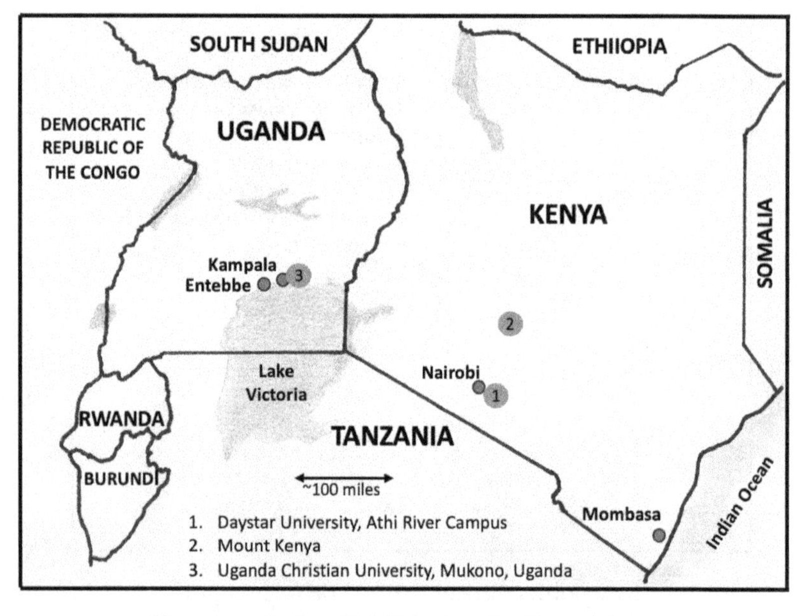

Key sites during Eddie's time in East Africa

11
Fear of Going to a Place I Call Home

"Home is the place that, when you have to go there, they have to take you in."

—Robert Frost

Unrest has been a staple within Liberia for decades, with two significant civil wars. These years of conflict have seen nearly one-third of the population displaced and have taken the lives of approximately 250,000 people. A prominent warlord turned Liberian President, Charles Taylor, ruled with violence at home and regionally. In 2003, as his government struggled under domestic and international pressure, the civil war entered Monrovia's capital. By late 2003, Taylor was forced to resign and sought asylum in Nigeria. While in Nigeria, Taylor attempted to escape and was arrested and extradited to the Hague to face charges of war crimes and crimes against humanity. In April 2012, the former Liberian president Charles Taylor was found guilty of aiding and abetting a notoriously brutal rebel force that murdered, raped, forced sexual slavery, built a child army, and mined diamonds to pay for guns. Taylor was then sentenced to fifty years in prison.

With Taylor's departure, a transitional government was established in 2003. Forces of the UN and the Economic Community of West African States Monitoring Group (ECOMOG) were positioned to keep the peace, and democratic elections were held in the fall of 2005. This resulted in the selection of Africa's first elected female head of state, President Ellen Johnson-Sirleaf, who had acquired an education in the United States at the University of Colorado Boulder and Harvard University, worked at the World Bank, etc. President Ellen Johnson-Sirleaf's job was formidable, governing a country with a weak or destroyed infrastructure, a primarily poor and under-educated population, and broad unemployment with little economic opportunity. The challenges notwithstanding, her election generated excitement and attention from the international community with solid domestic expectations for peace, development, and growth.

With peace restored, I was yearning to return to the place I called home. But was there a place to call home when all that made up my home was taken away from me by violence and conflict—my parents, my house, and my old friends? "Home" is a tricky concept to describe. It's a socially constructed idea, but it is a feeling that tells the story of ourselves. It reflects who we are and what we cherish in life. A house may be the bones of a home, but it can't capture the soul.

How could I find a home after feeling lost and uprooted from my parents and confined in a camp? It has been said that "home" is where the heart is. "Home" means so much more than just a house. So, how do we decide where home is? Over the past several years, as I have lived abroad, I've encountered this question: Where is home? Where do you call home? When asked this question, my simple answer has always been, "I am originally from Liberia," or sometimes I will say, "I was born in Liberia." When the name Liberia is mentioned, it is usually associated with Charles Taylor, war, destruction, even cannibalism. Often when I introduce myself as being from Liberia, I get the comment, "Oh, the home of Charles Taylor" or "The home of Samuel Doe—he was tortured by Prince Johnson," or "I hear the child soldiers killed people and ate their bodies and put the skulls on display!"

A country once described as a beautiful land of liberty and freedom and the beacon of hope to many from neighboring countries, had now become associated with evils and crimes. It has been vilified as the worst region in West Africa, and the most dangerous place to live and to travel. Be that as it may, it is still the place I identify as "home" even though I have not lived there since I was 17.

In 2005, the successful election of Madam Ellen Johnson-Sirleaf paved the way for Liberia to once again gain stability and recognition as a land inhabited by people of moral integrity, kindness, and goodwill. They were now hard-working and decent folks—people with dignity who respected the rule of law and loved living in peace and coherence. Her election also paved the way for Liberians living in the diaspora to return home.

One year after Ellen's election, I considered returning to Liberia to look for my parents and other family members whom I had not seen or made contact with for twenty years. The idea of going back got me thinking about the nature of "home" more seriously. It is no secret that individuals develop a strong emotional attachment to the places they've lived. These affectionate bonds between people and places go by a variety of names, including "rootedness," "attachment to place," and "established."[9] A solid attachment to the place where you live results in greater satisfaction with your home and expectations of future stability. These feelings transcend attachments to other people in the area and represent a genuine affection for the physical location. The passage of time strengthens our attachment to the places we live. Because our physical surroundings play an important role in creating a sense of meaning and organization in our lives, it is not surprising that our sense of the place we live is closely tied to our understanding of who we are.

In the movie, the "Wizard of Oz" young Dorothy Gale and her dog Toto are swept away by a tornado from their farm to the magical land of Oz. They embark on a journey with new friends to see the Wizard, who can return her to her home and fulfill the others' wishes. Dorothy doesn't achieve closure until she recognizes that "There is no place like home." Thus, the word "home" connotes more than just a house, but how exactly do we determine where "home" is? Having lived in several countries and interacted with many people of various social classes and backgrounds, I have always tried to understand where home was for me. When I had no option to go back to the place I called home, instead of languishing in the camp I embarked on the quest for education, which led me on a journey to multiple countries that brought a new perspective to the questions I asked earlier: where is home when you are a refugee confined in a camp in a foreign country? Where is home when you're lost, uprooted from your parents, and placed in a confinement camp? I firmly believe the answer to these questions is within you. I believe in the power of healing your wound with your own hands and with the support of trusted friends. The words of Mary Yuan speak truth to this: "The beauty of having a broken home is that it pushes you to dive deep into the meaning of home and try to find a way to rebuild it."[10]

As I traveled to seek new perspectives and knowledge, I was always viewed as an outsider who did not belong. Yet the feeling of being an outsider runs much deeper than religious brainwashing or being classed as one of the "unpopular kids" in school. This feeling of being an outsider looking in is something intrinsic, underground, and seemingly fundamental to my experience of being a human. Perhaps you've also carried this unshakable feeling within, that of being a nomad and wanderer. No matter how close you get to others, that feeling of being an outsider is always looming in the background—it's always present in your interactions with people, at least it has been with me. It is present in observations, desires, dreams, and motivations—and it awaits you at the beginning and end of your day. You know what I mean. And it's this very feeling that, in truth, has partially motivated me to share my story. I have asked the question over and over again: Why do I feel this way? Or, why do we think that we don't belong?

Simply put, at the core of feeling like an outsider looking in is the sense that something is not quite right. 'I don't belong because I can't relate to the people or environment around me; I don't look and speak like those around me.' I've experienced that all my life. I have experienced firsthand how isolating it can be when people look at you as an outsider looking in. It has been part of my journey. It has made me long for a home where I could feel completely understood, loved, and cherished. I have found that place in my soul, my wife, and my son. I am on a spiritual journey to search for my physical home.

I've also learned that being an outsider is a path in itself. I've come to embrace it and live it. I dare say that feeling like an outsider has been a crucial motivator in every aspect of my life in my search for my true home and to make sense of belonging. I've also learned to refuse what society taught us: being an outsider is a "bad" thing. So, I have to reframe what home is for me. "Home" is where I feel in control and correctly oriented in space and time; home is not a *place*, it's a *feeling*. It must be predictable and secure. I have also realized that a home can be rebuilt. In the words of poet Robert Frost, "Home is the place that, when you have to go there, they have to take you in." In short, "home" is the primary connection between you and the rest of the world.

The time had come for me to go to the place I referred to as "home." In September 2006, I embarked on the quest to locate my parents and family members since our separation from each other due to the Civil War in 1990.

According to Fretz and Shaw, "When violent conflict flares up, forced migration often follows. Ethnographic data shows that displaced people remain attached to their places of origin and often desire to return once conflict has abated, whether after weeks, months, or years."[11]

I can identify with this quote. I'd been barred from my native country for many years, and in all those years, my longing was always to return home one day. It was finally time to make that long-anticipated travel. My goal for going was to find my family, explore reconciliation and healing, dive deep, and explore the meaning of love and trust with people and places. But deep down in my heart, I had to deal with a fear of returning. I was afraid to return to my country and felt foreign. I was also scared that I might not belong in that society or encounter something that might affect my peacebuilding process. The landscape I left might have undergone radical changes through war and violence. I also feared that I might meet secondary occupants living in my childhood home or that it was destroyed in the aftermath of the war. I might also meet people working on our land. These ground-level realities might result in new forms of grief, threatening the peace I sought.

The country had gone through sixteen years of war—the infrastructure was destroyed; the institutions that ensured that citizens uphold the rule of law had collapsed; citizens were refugees in various countries, and many were internally displaced. You can understand my fear of going home after I'd been out of the country for many years. I experienced things others had not. Even if they had, whatever lessons they absorbed from their experience would be different from mine and vice versa. I had taken some local traditions from places I'd visited and made them my own, like wearing the "smock and Kente cloth" from Ghana or the "Kenzu" from Uganda, and eating a mashed banana with beans. I had been exposed to a new language and was learning to understand it (Kiswahili from Kenya and Twi from Ghana). I'd gotten used to doing things differently from how I had done them before leaving, and I was afraid this might alienate me. Of course, not belonging can be linked to feelings of worthlessness, isolation, self-doubt, and sadness. A sense of belonging has been described as one of our most essential needs. As Baumeister and Leary, M.R. say, "Belonging is "connectedness," or being "a part of something else."[12]

I had met a pastor who had brought his wife for medical treatment. As we started conversing about Liberia, he asked me about my parents. I told him I knew they were working in Firestone before the war, but I could not be together with them during the war, and I had escaped to Ghana and was now living in Nairobi. He promised that when he returned to Liberia, he would go to Firestone, find my parents, and email me. One day, I received an email from him: "Hi Eddie, I hope you're doing well. I managed to visit Firestone at Division #9 and met your brother. He and his family have returned from the refugee camp and are working at Firestone again. Sadly, he says that both of your parents died. He said they died from sickness and did not have access to treatment." After reading this email, I went numb, left the cybercafe, walked to the bus terminal, got a bus to my bus stop, and from there, I walked to my place and into my room. I broke down and cried for days.

I did not have any relatives with me; I was lonely. Knowing that I'd never again spend time with my parents was painful. It was in that state of grief and traumatic loss that I decided to return to Liberia to reconnect with other family members. I missed them dearly!

Getting ready to go home, I hoped not to feel distanced from my family and friends there. We'd grown in many ways; they had never been present in a single tiny aspect of my life living abroad—not graduation, birthday celebrations, Christmas, etc. I was also fully aware that if I wanted to belong, I had to be intentional about it and take the lead to reach out, because it takes courage and bravery to belong—that's what I had done living abroad, and I knew I could do it.

I boarded Brussels Airlines from Kenya across Africa, the Mediterranean, and Europe to Brussels. I had to fly to Europe from Kenya before going to Liberia because there were no direct flights between Uganda and Liberia, and Brussels Airlines and Air France were the only two airlines flying from Europe to Monrovia. The nonstop flight to Belgium was eight hours and twenty-five minutes long. Indeed, the view from the plane window did not disappoint. It has been shown that many factors influence our first-time impressions of people we meet and places we visit. The attributes used to describe a person—their clothing, their physical attractiveness, all strongly influence the first impressions we form. These impressions, in turn, influence subsequent behavior toward those people.

As I entered the terminal, it was crowded with high foot traffic, people moving to and fro, passengers going through security, some looking for their gate on the monitors while others were running to board their flight. As a newbie, the signage was essential for me at the airport as I navigated to the security check and then to my gate. Luckily, the signs were written in English, as it was in French, Dutch, and German. When I arrived at security, the line was long, and I immediately started panicking, with images of being late to my gate and missing my flight running through my mind. I was a slow-moving person in the airport security line, the frazzled, over-packed, discombobulated traveler woefully unprepared for the task. I became frantic and confused when I had to remove electronic devices from my bag and felt the wrath of the frustrated line of passengers behind me, anxious to get through security quickly. I finally went through security and found my way to my gate in time.

When it was finally time to board my flight, I said goodbye to Brussels. My nine-hour plane ride was very relaxing, and I sat next to a gentleman who was going to Sierra Leone. He was visiting for the first time since leaving his country due to Foday Saybana Sankoh's rebellion. Like me, he did not know where his parents were, and he was embarking on a journey to find them. We had a fascinating conversation. We talked about what it might be like in our war-affected countries. We both understood that the war had changed everything in our countries. Disasters could destroy homes, schools, and places of business and worship and disrupt the lives of people living in affected areas for a long time. Sometimes, people lost loved ones or experienced physical and mental injuries that might last a lifetime. Some people would experience a temporary or permanent loss of employment. Children being separated from family. Could we handle those changes when we got home to our respective countries? Returning home would be difficult and might be perceived as starting over again. However, there were ways to make such a transition more positive. I made up my mind to expect change. Failing to plan for changes can significantly contribute to the difficulties experienced. Hence, one should be ready to face changes in yourself, other people, places, and lifestyles due to the move and the effect of time.

We landed in Sierra Leone, and my friend said goodbye. I wished him all the best in his search to find his family. As we approached Monrovia, the pilot announced, "Get to your seats and buckle up. We are beginning our descent to Roberts International Airport." The airport and the entire city were in darkness, but our pilot managed to land the plane successfully. We disembarked from the plane, entered the terminal, and underwent security screening.

There were so many people, mostly airport employees and customs and immigration officers offering help, and in return, you would give them what is called "cold water." Cold water is a gift, or a gratuity given to a person when they have provided help. As a kind gesture of thanks, you provide "cold water." In Liberia, people say, "Here is cold water to cool your heart." When I saw all these people trying to help me, I knew the expectation, so I refused to get help! I wheeled my suitcases outside and stood waiting for the person coming to pick me up. Even there, I was surrounded by cab drivers asking to take me to my destination, but I was determined not to get help. They were murmuring among themselves, and I overheard some say, "He is a newcomer, and he is afraid of us." Indeed, I was afraid, and indeed, I was a newcomer and not knowledgeable about the social cues and social interaction between a cab driver and a passenger. I was also trying to protect myself from being robbed.

My ride finally arrived, and I was picked up, and we drove to Duport, where I stayed with my uncle Reverend Kotee and his family for a couple of months as he tried to help me trace my family. One of the things I tried to do was find similar people—those who'd had the same experience of leaving and returning once more, because they would understand my challenges.

When returning home, you are often confronted with rather lukewarm interest in your experiences abroad, precisely at a time when you want to share the rich experiences you have gained. However, it is difficult to grasp what it entails for family and friends back home who have yet to experience life abroad. So, finding a group with similar international experiences can be an excellent way to debrief, broaden your existing circle, and establish a new social circle.

After a couple of months of living in Monrovia, I started seeking friends whom I knew had returned home and were now living and working there. I contacted one of my colleagues from graduate school in Nairobi, who was then working with Samaritan's Purse International Relief. I visited his office, and we talked and reminisced about our college days. We connected and talked about how the brutal civil war that engulfed Liberia following Charles Taylor's invasion had left an indelible mark in the history of this West African country.

The fourteen-year Civil War struggle had led to the collapse of what was already an embattled economy; the near destruction of physical infrastructure built over a century and a half of enterprise and oligarchic rule; and to the killing, maiming, and displacement of 2.5 million Liberians. In Monrovia, I saw Liberia's beleaguered civilians in a new level of desperation. Disease and hunger had swept through crowds of internally displaced persons and many refugees returning to Liberia. The situation was highly chaotic and volatile, as many child soldiers and ex-combatants still had weapons with them and were waiting for an opportunity to once again use their weaponry.

Communication was complex, and the lack of public transportation severely curtailed movement around the city. Food and water supplies had become scarce, extensive looting had ravaged the neighborhood where I lived, there was widespread malnutrition, and tens of thousands did not have access to potable water and electricity. Liberians were still living in internally displaced facilities around the city. The conflict in Liberia was characterized by significant displacement and abduction. Thousands of women and girls lived away from their families and communities because they were abducted and served as the wives and cooks for the rebels.

In some cases, women chose not to return to their families or could not face the overwhelming burdens. Without skills, and in some cases without the financial support they had relied on during the war, either from being provided for by the faction to which they were associated or from looting, some women resorted to jobs such as prostitution, putting themselves at risk of more violence. Information gathered from child protection agencies in Lofa County indicated that prostitution was high after the end of the conflict, especially along the border areas between Liberia and Guinea.

In most cases, people could be seen walking by foot to the commercial district of Monrovia in search of food and employment. As a newcomer, I also joined the masses, walking under the scorching sun to places I wanted to go and visiting friends I wanted to see. While in Liberia, I met several other people with similar interests and experiences, which helped ease my frustration and displacement of being unable to connect with the people because I had become an outsider in my own country. As the Liberian economy imploded, poverty increased sharply, and more than seventy-five percent of Liberians now lived below the poverty line of one dollar per day. Unemployment and underemployment were high, as ex-combatants, returning refugees, and internally displaced persons needed help finding work and food. Refugees returning to their farms needed more seeds, fertilizers, tools, and, in some cases, had uncertain land ownership. Schools, hospitals, and clinics were severely damaged, and most government buildings were left in shambles. A generation of Liberians had spent more time at war than at school.

The longer I was in Monrovia, the more I started to acclimate to life, and I felt the need to stay longer and get involved in the nation's rebuilding process. I was then offered a position at Samaritan's Purse International Relief and Development as an Assistant Program Manager responsible for church rehabilitation, reconstruction, pastoral training, and facilitating and supervising road construction in rural Liberia. I was hesitant to accept the job offer because I had not intended to stay in Liberia but planned to search and find my family and then return to Kenya and be with my fiancée (I was engaged by then, which I will share about in another chapter). But when I saw the state of the country and the need for skills of educated Liberians to participate in the nation's rebuilding, reconciliation, and development, my heart was torn between staying and getting involved in the rebuilding process or leaving and joining my fiancée in Kenya. A couple of days after the job was offered, I requested my employer to give me a week to make my decision. During that one week, I contacted my fiancée, Lisa, and told her about the job offer and its implication on our relationship, particularly with the lack of a telecommunication network. After silence, she said, "Go ahead and accept the job. I will move to Liberia and support you." Wow! I was not expecting that response. I accepted the position, and in December 2006, Lisa visited for a week while enroute to the US from Kenya. This visit was crucial for Lisa to decide if she could see Liberia as a place she would like to live.

Following the inauguration of Ellen Johnson-Sirleaf, the new government faced the daunting task of rebuilding Liberia from the ashes of the war. It recognized that to be successful, it would need to implement policies aimed at both political stability and inclusive economic recovery that were mutually reinforcing. It would have to rebuild institutions and physical infrastructure and invest in human capacity through solid health and education programs to achieve sustainable development over time. Its initial strategy following the inauguration was articulated in its "First 150-Day Action Plan," which described in detail the steps it and the donor community would take between January and June 2006. This was followed by the development of an Interim Poverty Reduction Strategy (IPRS). The strategy had four fundamental pillars:

- Expanding peace and security.
- Revitalizing economic activity.
- Strengthening governance and the rule of law.
- Rebuilding infrastructure and providing essential services.

My work with Samaritan's Purse fell within the fourth pillar, 'rebuilding infrastructure and providing essential services.' We built roads and bridges in the inland areas to enable citizens to transport their goods for trade to larger cities. The domestic road network remains underdeveloped since the end of the war, and access to the country's northern and southeastern parts is limited, isolating it from the rest of the country.

We provided clean drinking water for residents in rural communities, giving community members a biosand filter to purify the drinking water they brought from the creek. During my work in the inland of Liberia, everyone I talked to, from market women to aid workers, underscored the importance of developing infrastructure in Liberia.

Additionally, the government and other non-profit organizations could only reach these places to deliver services and aid if there were good roads. Building better roads would help connect the country and open new economic opportunities. So, Samaritan's Purse International Relief and its partners funded several road renovation projects. We spent most of the time repairing roads to reach citizens living in villages, to deliver aid and provide clean water.

Once I was settled into my house and work, and I had access to reliable transportation, I began searching for my family living in Firestone Rubber Plantation, with the help of Reverend Kotee, who had been my mentor and host dad when I'd arrived in Liberia.

He took me to Firestone, Division #9, to search for my family. We met my brother and his wife and children, who had just recently returned from a refugee camp in Guinea. Everyone was shocked when they saw me get out of the car! I walked toward my brother and hugged him, and all of my nieces and nephews came around to greet me. They started narrating story after story about their escape from the rebels and how they had heard that I was dead. So, in memory of me, they'd given my name, Eddie, to one of my nephews. My brother told me the whole story about my parents; how they got very sick in the process of escaping and died in the refugee camp in Guinea. Then he shared a story of the soldiers, members of the Armed Forces of Liberia, going on their rampage, beating and torturing Firestone workers suspected of assisting Taylor's rebels. They raped women, forcing loved ones to watch. They dumped bodies in the Plantation's drainage ditches. The Plantation turned menacing and surreal; shadows darted through the rubber trees, corpses stuck out from weed-covered gutters, and artillery fire pounded like bass drums into the early hours of the night. He went on to say that neighbors turned on each other! One boy pointed NPFL soldiers to two workers from a targeted tribe, and Taylor rebels slit their throats. Three days later, the dead men's families handed over the boy to government soldiers. They executed him as well. "Nobody was there to protect the worker—nobody," he said. "The workers left with their children, their wives, everybody, nobody was left here, and when they left, that's the time the people started raising hell with us, so I took my family and started walking to Buchanan." He told story upon story, and I was becoming depressed from hearing those horrific tales.

After a moment of pause, I took the stage to tell the story of my escape from Monrovia to Ghana on a vessel. Hearing his stories made my escape to Ghana sound like much less a struggle and challenge. Regardless, we all had our troubles and impact from the war.

The following year, I got deeply involved with aid and development work in the Northern portion of Liberia in Gbarpolu County. Working in Gbarpolu posed a problem in my relationship with Lisa, as I could not communicate with her due to a lack of telecommunication services. I would have to walk several miles to a mountaintop to access the telecommunication signal to speak to her, and if we agreed on a particular time to call, I could walk to that location and wait for her call to come through. She lived in Nairobi then, and I was in the rainforest in Bopolu, Gbarpolu County.

Mobile and internet use was problematic because the network had limited penetration outside Monrovia. People needed to subscribe to one of three network providers: Lone Star, Cellcom, or Orange. And, in those early days, the service providers had not yet addressed the issue of international connectivity. I nearly resigned from my job to reunite with my fiancée because I could not handle the thought of being unable to talk to her as we were planning our wedding. However, we did successfully coordinate and plan our destination wedding.

A destination wedding requires careful planning (just like every other wedding). Couples planning to wed abroad face unique challenges as they plan their big day. For us, time differences interfered with our planning. Let's say you live in California but want to get married in Paris. You hop online, check out a few wedding packages from different venues, and find one that's everything you're looking for. Excited, you email the venue and ask to set up a meeting with their wedding coordinator. They're happy to oblige, but they're only available to chat at 10:00 a.m. Is that okay? Here's the thing; 10:00 a.m. in Paris is 1:00 a.m. in California. So, if you don't account for this time difference, you may miss out on chances to communicate with your wedding vendors. That was the case for us.

The second challenge for us was that not everyone we had hoped would attend could come. One of the best things about getting married (besides spending the rest of your life with your sweetheart) is celebrating with your friends and family. We did not have some of the very important people in our lives attend for various reasons, such as not being able to take time off from work, flights and hotels being prohibitively expensive, and some people with a fear of flying could not travel across the world to watch us say "I do." So, if you decide to have a destination wedding, it's very likely that some of your loved ones won't be there to celebrate in person. That's something you'll have to accept! But you can always find ways to include them, such as live streaming and phone calls, and posting real-time photos online for those who could not attend, while still enjoying the unique wedding ceremony you've dreamed of.

The other challenge about destination weddings is that your marriage might not be "official" in your eventual country of residence. We got married in Zanzibar, one of the most beautiful islands off the coast of Tanzania in East Africa, but little did we know that we would have a problem when it came to using our wedding certificate for legal purposes. When we were doing all the US immigration paperwork for me, and had to submit our marriage certificate, it was not officially recognized. Therefore, when we eventually traveled to the

US, we had to do a court ceremony to obtain an official US marriage certificate. Different countries have different laws for performing legal marriages, and at our wedding in Zanzibar, we had to have two ceremonies—one Islamic and one Christian. And some of the wording on the certificate was written in Swahili, the country's national language, making it difficult to interpret our marriage license for legal matters. We got married in Zanzibar on September 29, 2007, and right after our honeymoon we began our lives as a young couple by moving to the worst place to start our new life together—Liberia.

Prior to our arrival in Liberia, I had communicated with the Executive Director of the ELWA mission station, Les Unruh, to allow us to stay in one of ELWA's apartments. Les graciously offered us the apartment, but it was dilapidated and needed a facelift. We called it "The Bug House" because it was infested with many different sorts of bugs. There was no electricity or piped drinking water, so the first thing we had to do was buy a generator and hire an electrician to install a generator cable so we could have electricity in our apartment. We also had to purchase filters for our drinking and cooking water, and a fan to cool our bedroom to help us sleep at night because Liberia was so humid and hot, day and night.

Another challenge was mobility—we needed a car to go grocery shopping or go someplace for a getaway, so we decided to purchase a vehicle. At the time, buying a car in Liberia was not a luxury but a necessity. Because we did not have a really decent place in which to live, we became "house sitters" for missionaries and other expatriates living in Monrovia. We became known as professional house sitters, as we would live in other people's homes while they were away in order to maintain the household.

When we got a little more settled into our apartment and had somewhat of a routine, Lisa was offered a job as Grant Manager at

Samaritan's Purse, coordinating and managing a Global Fund grant for Orphans and Vulnerable Children (OVC) in two counties, Lofa and Montserrado. This project involved providing school fees for war orphans, distributing of mosquito nets, vocational training for caregivers, and education for the OVC, such as ensuring they were aware of paying their school tuition. Our jobs were very stressful, and the clients typically had a strong sense of "entitlement" by requesting "setting fees" or payments for their attendance at meetings and training sessions, which were provided for their benefit. Payment was even expected when a position was identified as a "volunteer," compounding the financial coordination with the US-based funding organizations. This entitlement stemmed from the fact that most of the people who provided these services had spent most of their time in refugee camps where everything was supplied to them by UNHCR. All of this caused us compassion fatigue on top of being very overwhelmed from being exposed to the trauma of others.

To make matters worse, we did not have a support system as a newly wedded couple, and we did not have a community—it was just me and Lisa. We were not even connected with our expatriate community at work. They assumed that I had my Liberian community because I was a Liberian. Little did they know that even though I was born in Liberia, I left as a teenager and had now returned after many years to try to reconnect and find healing for my trauma caused by the war. All my social networks and families were in different places, and I was still trying to make sense of the death of my parents during the war and trying to heal from that. Sometimes the office would organize an outing for the expatriates, but we would not be included, and we would only hear about it after the event had happened. That was our life for two and a half years in post-war Liberia.

People who have lost their original homes often find themselves lost and detached in a new environment. There is a loss in the sense of belonging and the feeling of being grounded that it embodied. Home is the physical manifestation of identity, security, a place of refuge, favorite family memories, and comfort. Over the years, I have tried to reconstruct or remake the perceived concept of my original home or reproduce some of its qualities, reestablishing a lost grounding and reclaiming my identity. That is why it is important to conceptualize the meaning of "home." I suggest an original framework to look at the concept of "home" from four different aspects: material; spatial; emotional; and imaginative, across which critical social processes or everyday activities are carried out.

1. Material aspect provides shelter, security, and the physical place for everyday activities, such as sleep, food preparation, consumption, etc.
2. Spatial aspect is the awareness of the physical dimensions of a home in terms of space, whether enclosed or the surrounding landscape. Spatial structure describes the space an individual navigates and occupies through everyday activities.
3. Emotional aspects comprise the sense of attachment, belonging, ownership, and the traumas inflicted by the loss of a home or the attempts to acquire the sense of attachment to a new home.
4. Imaginative aspects are narratives, images, or memories in a time-related dimension. These are memories of a home, whether lost or changed—the personal narratives of it, as well as the imaginary construct of an ideal home.

These four aspects and the social processes of everyday activities carried across them constitute the importance of home to its inhabitants and the possible pathways that may be engaged to recreate and adapt a new place to include a fragment of the old, which is argued to foster a sense of attachment and integration into the new environment. No place like home exists, regardless of how long one has lived abroad in a particular domain; there will always be a longing for home.

12
The Story of Us!

"Place me like a seal over your heart, like a seal on your arm; for love is as strong as death, its jealousy unyielding as the grave. It burns like blazing fire, like a mighty flame. Many waters cannot quench love; rivers cannot sweep it away. If one were to give all the wealth of one's house for love, it would be utterly scorned."

–Song of Solomon 8:6-7

Rather than "love at first sight," I would say it was *recognition* at first sight. This is the story of how I met my wife, Lisa. The story began in 2000, at Daystar University in Nairobi, Kenya, where I studied. I was among the students picking up a group of American students at Jomo Kenyatta International Airport, Nairobi. who had come on a study abroad program at the university. After several hours of waiting, the airport monitors finally announced the plane's arrival from Amsterdam. We stood at the arrival point with our posters reading, "Welcome to Daystar!"

As the passengers made their way out, I saw this beautiful girl wearing blue track pants with white stripes. I was instantly captured by her, and I whispered to my colleague, "That girl is gorgeous!" She kept walking toward the Daystar poster, and I asked, "Are you one of the students?"

"Yes," she replied.

I offered my hand, and said, "My name is Eddie. What's yours?"

"Lisa," she replied. "Nice to meet you." She gently shook my hand and then walked to join her fellow students.

I reiterated to my friend, "She's beautiful!" We both laughed about it and gathered their luggage. We loaded the coaster (bus) and headed to the university. On our way, my friend confirmed what I had said about this girl by saying, "Yes, you're right, she's one of the most beautiful girls." We laughed again, and everyone on the coaster wondered why.

The semester started, and we settled into the routine of attending lectures. Over the course of the semester, Lisa and I got to know each other a little better. I would now call her by her name and we'd have casual conversations. I would sometimes accompany her early in the morning when she would call home to her parents from the only telephone booth on campus. I sometimes asked her to help me type my papers, since I was slow at typing. Our friendship started to grow, and, as we had some mutual friends on campus, we would sometimes hang out together.

Over the course of the semester, we became good friends. We would meet in the International Student Office with my Kenyan friend, who also worked with international students, to talk and reminisce about the experience at the airport. We laughed at how scared American students always were when they arrived in Africa for the first time—you could tell them to do anything, and they would do it without question!

As the semester continued, our friendship grew. We went to the city together, had lunch together, and I accompanied her to an orphanage in one of the slum areas of Nairobi, in which she had supported a child for several years. All this time together made each of us further enjoy the other's company. As the semester drew to a close, the international students usually made a trip to climb Mount Kenya, to Point Lenana at an elevation 16,355 feet. The climb sometimes took four to six days to reach the peak, depending on the route and the fitness level of the group. During that semester, Lisa's group of students decided to take the expedition.

It was a program tradition that regular Daystar students who worked with the international students would accompany the American students on the trip. During this semester, I was one of the students selected to go with the American students as a guide. Being on this trip further solidified our friendship and helped me to get to know Lisa better in a different setting and under challenging circumstances.

Mount Kenya is the highest mountain in Kenya. It is the second highest in Africa, standing 17,057 feet high. Mount Kenya has three summits: Batian, Nelion, and Point Lenana. Despite being a stratovolcano, the peak's rough appearance is due to its past covering of ice. Near the top, there remain small glaciers. Mount Kenya National Park encompasses the region surrounding the peak and is noted for its diverse vegetation and animals. As one climbs higher on the mountain, the vegetation changes from lowland savannah to bamboo forests. The unusual high-altitude equatorial habitat is also found there. With the odd flora and the foggy conditions, the scenery seems to belong to another beautiful world. The routes to the three main summits are rugged, steep, and challenging, requiring ample preparation, a considerable level of fitness, and the services of an experienced guide.

Was I prepared? No! Were the students sufficiently prepared for the climb? Definitely not! All we did was hire the assistance of a professional guide, a cook, and trained first aid personnel. The more we trekked toward Point Lenana through the rocky trails, the more we experienced altitude sickness, fatigue, and headaches.

By day two, most of the students were not feeling well, and as a student leader on the trip with limited experience in mountaineering, I started wondering if we would, or should, complete the journey. As we began day three, I prayed that today would be better than yesterday, and I asked Lisa if she would allow me to help her carry her backpack. At first, she hesitated and said "You've got your backpack, too. How will you hold the two bags?"

I insisted that I wanted to help, and a colleague, Alex, made fun of her: "Baughman!" he called her (by her maiden name) laughing, "Let him help you!"

She replied, "You don't have to, but if you want to, that is fine." So, we made a brief stop and I put my stuff into her big backpack and put it on my back, and we continued, trying to catch up with the rest of the team. As we approached them, I noticed some of the girls were limping from blisters.

Nevertheless, we did make it to our next camp site. Everyone was exhausted, but our cook was busy, full of energy, making us food and telling stories about climbing Mount Kenya. Some of our team members even went to bed before the meal was ready and had to be awakened in order to eat. At the end of this day, I started experiencing body aches and soreness, but I still had enough energy to continue.

We woke up on day four, and everyone was still feeling pretty tired. We had our breakfast and team talk, and our guide told us that our journey today would take us to the base of Point Lenana. Then early the next morning, we would climb to the summit. I was excited to hear that, but wondered how rocky and steep it was going to be, how the high altitude would affect us, and how many hours it would take us to get to the base, called Shipton's Camp.

After breakfast, we walked to Shipton's Camp through the valley, crossing a couple of creeks. We walked for seven or eight hours, stopping several times to eat, drink, and enjoy the views. The climb to the base of Point Lenana was a brutal stretch—the ground was covered with snow, the temperature was cold, we encountered rain and wind, and hiked at a plodding pace.

We finally reached Shipton's Camp at 5:00 p.m., we ate our dinner, and each person went to bed immediately for some needed rest for the final leg of the climb.

The next morning, we woke up at 2:00 a.m., had tea and bread, packed our backpacks, and started our ascent to the Lenana summit. The plan was to get there before sunrise at 6:30 a.m. This final leg of the climb was by far the hardest slog, and the path consisted of rugged terrain that cut through the cliff toward Point Lenana. It was a struggle for everyone, but we all reached the top and saw the sunrise! It was a breathtaking moment mixed with joy and tears.

After taking it all in, we hiked down and made our way to Daystar. What an experience that was! It remains one of the craziest experiences I have ever had, and it allowed me to bond with Lisa and casually talk about what was next after graduation.

I asked her what her plan was after graduation. "Hum! I don't know yet, but I am hoping to go to graduate school," she said.

"What do you want to pursue a master's degree in?" I asked.

"I plan to attend Washington University in St. Louis at George Warren Brown School of Social Work" she responded. She also asked me about my parents' whereabouts and if I was in contact with them or had heard about where they might be. "Unfortunately, I've not heard from them or know their whereabouts since I left Liberia in 1990."

"Do you miss them?" she asked. "Yes, I do, but I've no way of getting in contact." She was shocked to hear that I had been separated from my parents for that long. The look on her face told me that she was feeling sad and compassionate for me.

I also felt sympathetic when she told me that she would miss her graduation ceremony because of her being in Africa. It was sad for me because graduation is such a significant milestone—after rigorous academic work in college, you want to celebrate your accomplishments with friends and family. So, I was sad that she wouldn't get to do that or have photos to remind her of the event.

At the end of the semester, the consortium of international students left for a debrief retreat at Lake Navaisha. Before they left, I met with my friend Alex Jami, who encouraged me to talk with Lisa about my feelings. He also asked if, while at the retreat, he could "investigate" to see if she felt the same way toward me.

When they returned to campus, Alex told me I needed to talk to Lisa that very night and let her know how I felt about her, because she would be heading to Mombasa to visit her roommate the next day and then return to the US.

I walked to her dormitory and asked the security lady on duty if she would allow me to see Lisa, and I gave her Lisa's room number. She went in to look for Lisa and returned to let me know that Lisa was not in the room, but she'd left a message with her roommate telling Lisa that I was looking for her. I walked back to my room feeling very nervous and thinking about how to start the discussion if she came.

Thirty minutes later, I heard a knock on my window. "Who is that?" I asked.

I heard a voice saying, "Lisa."

I came out of my room, and we walked toward the Student Center and sat under a tree. I asked her questions about her experience here and what the reentry process would be like for her. We had so much to talk about, and eventually she said, "Alex told me you wanted to say something to me." I finally 'spilled the beans' and told her I loved her and wanted us to date.

There was a moment of pause, she acknowledged the courage it took for me to tell her about my feelings, and then asked, "How can you say you love me, when you don't even know me?"

I thought through that question in my mind, but my other thought was that she was indirectly telling me that she was not interested, or perhaps she was in doubt about me and didn't know what to do with my expression of love for her.

I responded, "You are right, but I want to get to know you better because of that fact. We can try and see."

She said, "I've never been in a long-distance relationship, and you add cultural layers to it, making it even more challenging. Besides, I am unsure if I will be back in Africa, and therefore, I cannot commit to a relationship. Let us continue to be friends and communicate and leave the door open." We concluded on a good note with a mutual understanding of the situation. We prayed, and I walked her to her hostel.

The following day, Lisa left for Mombasa with her roommate and left me with a suitcase that she would not need for the trip. While in Mombasa, her passport was stolen. She returned to Nairobi, canceled her flight to the US, filed a police report, and then took the report to the US Embassy to apply for an emergency travel document.

I escorted her to the embassy but stopped far from the building for fear that as an African, I might be suspected of being a spy for

Al-Shabaab, the Somali militant group! Lisa rescheduled her flight for the next day, hoping to get a new passport and leave.

After forty-five minutes in the embassy, she came out with a piece of paper requiring that a US-approved passport photo be taken. We didn't have much time, so we quickly made our way into the city, had photos taken at a studio, and rushed back to the embassy.

Lisa presented her photos, and she was then told they did not meet the criteria. By this time, it was getting late, offices were closing, and we thought that most likely the embassy would be closed by the time we returned from the city. But once again, we went to the road to wait for a taxi or minivan to take us to the next station where we could get yet another one into the city. After waiting awhile without getting a vehicle, we decided to walk toward the nearest taxi station. Time was our biggest enemy, and I kept looking at my watch as we walked. Midway to the taxi station, we got a minivan that took us to the next station, and we luckily got another van that needed just two passengers to fill up. We got into the busy, crowded part of Nairobi, looking for the better photo studio, and I kept asking others if they knew where the studio was. We finally found the studio to take the photos but realized that returning by public transportation would take too long, and by the time we got to the embassy it might be closed. So, we hired a cab to drive us to the embassy, wait for us, and then drive us back. Lisa came out of the embassy with her passport in her hand, smiling. We got in the car, and it took us to Lisa's youth hostel. She packed her bags, said goodbye, and left for the airport, closing that chapter of our time together.

A few days later, I received an email saying she had arrived safely, and she thanked me for everything. That was the beginning of many emails and 'snail-mail' communications. I also wrote back and said

I was glad that everything had gone well, and that I was pleased I could be there to support her.

We exchanged emails and letters for four years, and in 2004 Lisa returned to Nairobi to visit her former roommate. We reconnected, chatted, and reminisced about the experience of her lost passport and laughed. It was great to see her again because I'd thought it might never happen. I remember sitting with her in a restaurant in downtown Nairobi as her two-week visit was ending, thinking that I should revisit our conversation from 2000. I eventually got the courage and asked, "Have you thought more about our discussion in Daystar prior to your departure? What new thoughts do you have?"

She looked me and said, "Nothing has changed. We still have the same obstacles we had when we talked four years ago… you are still here, and I am in the US, and as I said, I don't want to have a long-distance relationship."

We concluded the conversation on that note and ate our lunch. Her visit ended, and we went back to exchanging emails and letters.

One day in 2005 she had exciting news. "I am coming back to Nairobi and will be working with the International Justice Mission (IJM)."

"Wow!" I said. "When are you coming?"

"Soon," she said, "I have to go to IJM headquarters in DC for orientation and training first, and then I will be coming to Nairobi."

I was so excited to hear she was coming and that we could live in the same city. If there's a story that proves true love stands the test of time, it's ours.

In 2005, Lisa arrived in Nairobi, and since we lived close, it was easy to talk, go out, do fun things, and communicate without obstacles. It even made talking about relationship and dating less awkward and intimidating.

Finding true love is an amazing feeling, but it is even more incredible when you find it after waiting and struggling for months and years together. When I think of our love story and the many years of waiting, it reminds me of the two Biblical characters, Jacob and Rachel. Jacob was so impressed and fascinated by Rachel's beauty and enchanted by her charm that he was willing to work and wait many years for marriage. We too, spent a lot of our time waiting. Waiting in line. Waiting for news. Waiting for a response. Waiting for a promotion. Waiting for the next season of life.

God is at work in our waiting. We might not see any changes in these times of waiting, particularly through times of difficulty and periods of personal growth, but there is a plan and purpose in all of it. God can see things that need to be ironed out in our hearts and our lives that would only remain creased and messy if it weren't for the refining times of waiting.

To those who may be waiting, whether through a long, drawn-out process in your personal life or anything else, I want to encourage you that God is in your waiting and is working everything for your good, and your waiting will turn out to be worth it at the end.

I learned many lessons that strengthened and fortified my faith during my waiting process. I am not just talking about waiting for that special girl to say "Yes." Apart from waiting for Lisa, I was also waiting for something else significant—the civil war to end in my country, Liberia, so I could return and hopefully find my family. Through my time of waiting, I learned four valuable lessons that I want to share with you with the hope that they will be useful to you when you encounter a waiting period:

1. Waiting keeps you in a humble position, seeking God's face to hear His direction.
2. Waiting taught me that what I *want* is not necessarily what I *need*. God had His plan, and He was working out His plan quite differently from what I wanted.
3. Waiting encourages you to appreciate God, family, and friends. While waiting in Kenya, I drew closer to God, and I created intimate relationships. I also learned to appreciate the importance of family. I would wake up on many days and wish I had my family with me. Lastly, I developed and built genuine friendships, and some of them are still part of my life.
4. Waiting strengthens you to endure when life is not going your way. When life was tough for me in Nairobi and my colleagues were moving to the next chapters of their careers or going to graduate school, I decided to stay in Nairobi until God opened a path for me.
5. Waiting empowers you to embrace challenges as invitations to think "outside the box," pushing your creative boundaries and discovering new facets of your potential.

On September 29, 2007, seven years after we had met, we had a magical beach wedding ceremony on the island of Zanzibar, Tanzania, at the Shooting Star resort, on the beautiful sandy white beach on the blue Indian Ocean. Having a fun wedding on the beach was a true fairy tale and a dream come true. Most importantly, having our loved ones and friends cheering as we took our first steps towards a brand-new life brightened everything and made it extra special. Lisa's parents and some of Lisa's best friends made the long trip to Zanzibar to attend the ceremony. I also had some of my friends from Kenya, US, Liberia, and Sierra Leone attending.

A few years later, we embarked on a journey to adopt, as it was our desire when we got married. Our country of choice was Uganda because we were already living and working there. When we began this journey, I was unaware that fraud and deceit were at the heart of Uganda's adoptions to the United States. Uganda families had been bribed, tricked, or coerced into giving up their children to Westerners for adoption. It also became apparent that it was a lucrative industry in Uganda in which lawyers, acting on behalf of foreign applicants, received large payments to process all the adoption paperwork as quickly as possible. While I didn't expect it to be all sunshine and rainbows, neither did I realize the depth of heartache and loss that adoption can entail, not only for adoptive parents but even more so for the adopted child, like the one we were to meet and welcome into our lives. Lisa and I thoroughly researched each step of the process to ensure a proper and ethical adoption, and we were prepared to follow the correct procedures and processes. We were introduced to an agency that aligned with our values and beliefs regarding adoption, and they guided us every step of the way. For us, adopting was about sharing the love and home that God had given us with a child whom He loved and cared about and to whom He wanted for us to be his earthly parents.

The new adoption laws enacted in Uganda in 2016 resulted in a more challenging adoption process to navigate. One of the main challenges that foreign families must meet is the residency requirement of fostering child in Uganda. Prospective adoptive parents must live in Uganda for three years before the process can be finalized, and the prospective adoptive child is supervised by the probationary district social worker for a minimal of one year before an adoption can be approved by the Ugandan authorities. So, we had to live in Uganda for three years to foster and adopt. Luckily, we worked and lived in Uganda, so meeting the residency requirement was not a problem for us in this journey. However, it was challenging when we could not travel with our child outside of Uganda until the adoption was finalized. In 2016, we welcomed a handsome, strong, intelligent, and brave ten-month-old boy named Ezekiel into our home. Although the Uganda adoption was completed, we could not travel with Zeke. We first had to obtain a Ugandan passport for him and then apply for a US visa.

Uganda is not a part of the Hague Convention, which means that certain restrictions prevented our son from immigrating to the United States as a citizen. However, he could enter the US as a non-immigrant, referred to as the B-2. We, therefore, obtained a B-2 visa for Zeke to come to the US with us. After our arrival in the US, I had a doctor's appointment and was soon diagnosed with cancer (multiple myeloma) and we were then unable to return to Uganda to complete the US adoption paperwork. As a result, we started a new chapter of adoption paperwork in the US. We hired an attorney specializing in immigration law, in all areas related to children's immigration issues, to help us complete Zeke's adoption paperwork in the US. We were grateful to have gotten someone knowledgeable in international and domestic adoption to work with us every step until Zeke became naturalized as a US citizen.

My wife is my soulmate—she accepts my many faults and puts up with my flaws daily. We complement each other, and I realize I couldn't go through this life, this crazy journey, without her. If everything I have today was taken from me and I was left with just my wife and son, I would be perfectly fine. This bond between us can never be replicated, broken, or dulled. The only change I've seen in that bond is that it has become stronger and more passionate over the years—something I wouldn't have believed possible during our puppy love phase. She shares my passion and supports me in everything. Next to God's Grace, my wife Lisa is the greatest gift in my life, but if I had followed my plan, I would never have met her!

To my wife:

Lisa, you have driven me crazy with love since I first took the time to get to know you, and I realized you're just as beautiful on the inside as you are on the outside. And I can't wait for you to continue driving me crazy until one of us takes our last breath. You're worth the seven years of waiting! I am glad I waited for God's timing and did not follow my plan. You are my best friend! I love you, sweetheart.

If you're at a crossroads in life, please pray and seek the intervention of God before you take the next step. "That perfect plan" you have might be the wrong one.

Remember that God loves you, and His plans for you are perfect. When He closes a door, it's only because He wants to open a better one! Even if you have stepped off course, remember that His Grace is bigger than your biggest mistakes! Trust Him to redirect you back to His perfect plans. "For I know the plans I have for you," declares the Lord, "Plans to prosper you and not to harm you, plans to give you hope and a future." (Jeremiah 29:11). I hope that you will be encouraged by these thoughts.

13

Refugee Memories: Visit to My Former Refugee Settlement in 2007

The mid-twentieth-century refugee catastrophe and the ongoing mass statelessness problem exposed the deathly frailty of the Western political and human rights project. Today, more than 21 million people live a vulnerable and marginalized existence in refugee camps and settlements. I lived in such a settlement camp in Ghana for eight years thirty-three years ago. I arrived at the settlement in September 1990 and left in 1998 for my undergraduate degree in Kenya.

In 2007, I visited the Buduburam Refugee Camp with my wife, having been gone for ten years. I left the camp in 1998 for Nairobi, Kenya for my undergraduate studies and then lived in Kenya for eight years before moving back to Liberia in 2006. I wanted my wife to see where I had lived most of my teenage and young adult life. The camp had become like a settlement, with several permanent structures. All the tents had been replaced with makeshift structures. However, I saw many people I knew who were still living in the camp. Although it had been ten years since I left the center, images of donors' fluttering flags still marked it, and various international organizations' bold branding was still visible. Additionally, securing life's necessities remained out of reach for residents. Inadequate sanitary conditions and general well-being had worsened.

The termination of the refugee status and the removal of UNHCR's support in Buduburam

Buduburam camp residents are like travelers waiting for a flight whose destination is unknown. Liberia conducted an election in 1993, which brought Madam Ellen Johnson-Sirleaf into power, and the United Nations deemed it fair enough to allow for a safe homecoming. As a result, the UNHCR stopped providing refugee aid to Liberians in Ghana and the settlement lost a lot of assistance. Approximately 3,000 refugees returned to Liberia at the time, but most people opted to stay in Ghana, and the Buduburam village remained the heart of their society.

At the time of our visit, the camp was at a critical juncture. In a UNHCR bulletin posted around the camp in 2007, residents were notified of the imminent closure and repatriation of residents, setting off a panic. As I spoke with residents on the issues, I found that most people feared and opposed repatriation because of the unknown. The other camp residents I spoke with assessed the prospect of returning by evaluating their capabilities to meet the known demands of living in Ghana, in contrast to the unknown or perceived needs of moving back to Liberia. Many people expressed nostalgic longings for the comforts of their former homes in Liberia but saw little chance of resuming life as it had been, should they choose to go back.

Liberia had changed. Their families were gone. Their villages had been burned or destroyed. Though they were not happy in Ghana, only a few saw the possibility of becoming happy if they were to repatriate. Most people felt that staying was more advantageous than returning. Staying appeared more economically feasible, despite the difficulty of sustaining livelihoods in the camp. Staying also seemed safer.

Return as Economically Unfeasible

Most camp residents saw the return as a setback, rather than an improvement to their economic situation. I quickly understood that the longer Liberians remained in exile, the more complicated it would be to return. Most residents I spoke with were unwilling to sacrifice the roof over their heads, the scholarships for their children's education from NGOs, or the meager subsistence they had established at Buduburam.

What was central in all my conversations with the residents was their inability to imagine a stable economic situation for their family. Most people still needed help in seeing their way through the day. The phrase "finding food" was often used to denote the inconsistency of sustenance for most families, as the phrase is normally used to describe someone or something that is desperately looking for food.

For post-conflict governments like the one in Liberia, returning Internally Displaced Persons (IDPs) and refugees were often seen as a means of nation-building. But the Liberians in Buduburam were less inclined to see their return as a citizenship and nation-building opportunity so much as a means of personal or family development.

Since the growth prospects were unforeseeable, none of the residents I spoke with were interested in repatriation.

Insecurity

Insecurity was something that was brought out in my conversations. What the camp residents imagined was the insecurity they would face if they were to return to Liberia. Most of the residents and/or their families had encountered severe violence and loss as a result of the civil conflict in Liberia. Many feared their past encounters with government or rebel troops would result in further trouble upon their return, since former child soldiers lived in the community. Each one of us Liberians who'd escaped from our country felt the same way. The life-threatening environments and traumatizing events we'd been exposed to redefined our perception of, and our relationship to, our country. After spending eight years in Kenya, I too had struggled with the decision to return home, and did so only after I heard the news of the death of my parents.

The suffering of being a young man without parents was unbearable. I didn't know how to cope. Move on or "survive." Some days, I did not know what to do. As time went on, I realized that this grief was unbearable, and it was quite possibly the hardest thing I would ever go through. I grieved that they were not physically part of the significant events in my life, like getting married. I wished they could have attended my wedding and met my wife, but I hope they will see me and tell me they were with me, someday. That they will tell me they sat on the beach and watched me marry my wife. I wish they could meet my son, their grandson. We could have shared laughter and snuggles together with my baby boy.

I could genuinely understand the plight of my fellow Liberians in the camp. Given the severe brutality of fourteen years of civil war and political unrest, it is little wonder that we would feel apprehensive about returning to face the reality of hearing the sad news of the death of their loved ones or not having anything to go back to.

In many ways, life at Buduburam strongly resembled the way of life for others throughout the world who have lived in enclaves of poverty. This impoverished struggle is typical in protracted refugee situations throughout Africa and worldwide. These Liberian refugee families struggled to survive with few resources. Many refugees who have remained in the camp for decades were deemed "safe," and the repatriation program has failed to sufficiently engage with and understand the concerns of the refugees in the context of return. Those who have not experienced a protracted life in exile cannot fully understand the reluctance to return.

My visit deeply reminded me of my experience living there, triggering my anxiety disorder, depression and post-traumatic stress disorder (PTSD). While traumatic events can occur at any age, those that occur during childhood can be especially important, with the potential for more significant and long-lasting impacts.

14
The Punitive US Visa Application Process

"An ordinary African trying to visit a European Nation is like trying to milk an elephant because of the visa process. However, for a European to visit an African Nation is like a walk on the beach, like going to have a cup of tea..."

—Dr. Alfred N. Mutua,
Kenya Foreign Affairs Minister.

This chapter reviews my interactions with the US embassy as I attempted to get an F-1 (student visa) and B-1 (visitor visa) on separate occasions over a one-year period. It does not necessarily follow the sequence or chronological order of the other chapters. Nevertheless, I will lay out the series of events as they occurred and provide my critical analysis of why many people from the African continent are denied visas to enter the United States. You will also notice that some of the discussions might overlap.

I was born in Liberia, but the endless war forced me to leave in 1990 for Ghana and register with the United Nations High Commission for Refugees (UNHCR) as a refugee. As a refugee,

I often applied for resettlement to a third country, but the requirements usually disqualified me. The condition used at the time was that you had to know someone in the country you were attempting to go to, and that individual had to apply for you, attesting that he, she, or they would be responsible for all your expenses and well-being while you were living abroad. I gave up and felt hopeless when I did not meet this minimum requirement. Nonetheless, I still wanted to explore other options—the Green Card or Diversity Green Card visa lottery.

I applied for the Diversity Immigrant Visa Program (Green Card Lottery) in Ghana. It is a US immigration program that seeks to increase the relative number of immigrants from countries with proportionately low levels of immigration to the United States. It would allow you to live and work in the United States, but the US government would not pay for your airfare, find you a place to live, or find you work. As part of your application, you would have to prove that you were unlikely to become dependent, or a "public charge" on the US government for living expenses. That is, you had to demonstrate that you could support yourself, and strongly convince the US immigration authorities that you would not need to rely on government assistance in the United States. Once again, this was an obstacle for me! I did not have sufficient proof of financial self-sufficiency or evidence of assets to meet the qualifications. My best bet would be for a friend or family member to volunteer to sponsor me, in which case they would need to file an affidavit of support... none of which I had.

So, I also gave up hope on that dream and turned to seeking opportunities for school in Ghana. I remained in Ghana, completed my high school education, and proceeded to Kenya to continue my college education. I applied to Denver Seminary in the United States while completing my undergraduate degree and was offered admission and given a fifty percent tuition scholarship. I was extremely excited about going to "the land of milk and honey" where dreams are realized, but I needed to raise the remaining fifty percent. I solicited support for the remaining tuition from friends, and my Form I-20 Certificate of Eligibility for Nonimmigrant student status was sent to me.

I then moved swiftly to apply for an F-1 visa, and, luckily for me, I was given an earlier interview appointment (typically, with the visa backlog, people had to wait a month or two for an appointment). Sadly, I was refused my first visa interview based on insufficient proof of intent to return home after completing my academic studies. I tried to plead my case, but I was not given the opportunity. I left the embassy feeling extremely dejected and depressed. Nonetheless, I did not give up; I reapplied for a second interview and requested the seminary to send me a new admission letter and an I-20 certificate. I applied for a visa interview, paid my hundred-dollar application fee, and was given an interview date and time.

There I was, back at the American Embassy for a second interview, in July 2006. The man who interviewed me the last time was on the left, a burly man was in the middle, and an elderly lady with white hair was on the right. I moved ahead in my queue, but I noticed that not a single visa was granted to any of those ahead of me in line. My turn. The man who interviewed me the last time was free, so I walked up to him—I didn't like this coincidence. Of course, he didn't remember me, but when he started typing, my information appeared on his screen. He glanced at me.

"Is this your second interview?"

"Yes."

"Go to counter seven, please."

I stepped aside and asked a guard where counter seven was. He pointed at the burly man in the middle, and someone was leaving his counter. I had my documents, but he didn't ask for them, and I didn't dare show him anything until he asked. He asked for my invitation letter and his questions were the same as last time: the purpose of the trip and the funding source. He added another question: "How much do you earn?" He contorted his face when I told him where I worked and how much I earned. At the time, I worked for a church in Nairobi and tried to save as much as possible for something like this. "Are you going to pay for your education?" he continued.

"Yes." I picked up my scholarship letter and showed him. He paused his typing. I was thinking: "Dude, I've been saving, and I've been working. Plus, I didn't fall from the sky. I have people who can help me if I ask for help."

"Are you married?"

"No."

He shook his head. "Do you have any children?"

"No." He shook his head more vigorously this time. I stood there wondering what he was up to. He walked away from his desk and into the embassy somewhere. It left me wondering whether he was consulting with someone else about my case. I was thinking, *Here comes the curse of the young, unmarried male without kids. I know what's coming next.*

He returned, sat at his desk, and opened his computer. "Have you traveled before?"

"Yes."

"Where?"

I mentioned the countries.

He listened keenly before speaking. "I'm sorry, but I can't issue you a visa. It is tough to travel to the United States unless you have traveled out of Africa before." At that moment, I was boiling with anger. He said, "On this yellow piece of paper, you will find the reason..." and that reason was that I didn't have sufficient proof that I would return. It was like a scene from the movie, *The Terminal*—except that the Tom Hanks character is trapped in the airport for nine months, whereas this story played out at the American Embassy in just five minutes, and I was trapped in Africa. I walked away like a man in a trance. Embassies make much money off visa applications and Africa is estimated to lose $50 million in rejected visa applications to the West annually. The default mode at the US Embassy is "Reject."

Maybe they thought I wanted to go to the US, burn my Liberian passport, start seeking asylum, or marry an American citizen and change my status and remain there. I thought of all the impoverished Liberians and Kenyans I knew who had told the most blatant lies, presented the greatest fake documents at the American Embassy, and were given visas. I thought too, of Liberians and Kenyans with strong financial muscle and bulky bank accounts who intended to travel to the US to engage in businesses, do academic work, or to holiday and return, but were rejected visas. Sometimes the consular officers knew that the person they were interviewing would never return, yet they still issued a visa, whereas another person who would have returned, was rejected.

Once again, I was denied based on not having strong "ties that bind" me to my country of origin. Strong ties differ from country to country, city to city, and individual to individual. In my case, strong ties would have been a family, a bank account, social and family relationships, and possessions, that would bind me to my country of residence or birth. When I was applying, I was a single man from a war-ravaged country living in a country that was not my country of birth. The decision as to whether or not I qualified for a visa was primarily based on an assessment of my situation.

Since my case had remained the same, the decision was unlikely to change. However, I reapplied again for the third time, but the issue at stake this time was that I needed to provide new evidence demonstrating my ties to my country. I was in a dilemma, I could not establish strong ties to Liberia since it was at war, nor could I provide new evidence showing solid ties to Kenya because I was there temporarily as a student. I couldn't explain the significant change in my circumstances with further information not presented during the previous interview(s) that would change my status. So, I just honestly presented my case, the accompanying documentation, and the facts. But it was not convincing enough for the consular officer, and I was denied. I told myself this was my last attempt because the process was tedious. When applicants reapply, they must submit a new application, pay the application fee, and schedule a new appointment. Another consular officer not previously associated with your case would conduct an "unprejudiced" interview and decide independently after considering your circumstances. For me, I did not have luck with any attempt I made. I was honest in my responses to the consular officer's questions, and I was trying to go to the US with good intentions but was always denied. I met every requirement for the F-1 visa, such as (1) being a legitimate student, (2) having the ability to cover the cost of my education and living in the US, for which I had documentation, and (3) having strong ties to my home country and planning to return after completion of my studies.

While I was being denied a visa to enter America with all of my genuine documents, others were being interviewed who had falsified records, even gotten fake bank account statements that indicated they had sufficient money in their account, gave documentation to prove they owned property, etc. They were given their visas, and I was denied.

The visa interview environment in Nairobi was dehumanizing. All applicants were placed in an open space with a telephone through a tiny opening. The interviewer sat behind a glass window and spoke to you through the phone. As you responded, all your fellow applicants could hear your conversation, and whether you were denied or accepted entry to the US. There was no privacy or human dignity for an interviewee. They talked to you so unkindly and were demeaning and very intimidating. This humiliating process gave me a glance into the immigration process in the United States. We live in a time in which we are faced with a social inequity crisis, whereby those who have, treat those who don't with discontent and disrespect, which was representative of the actions of the consular officers at the US Embassy in Nairobi.

Having been dismissed in Nairobi multiple times for an F-1 visa, I was invited by a friend's brother, a youth pastor, to attend a conference in the United States to speak on the prevalence of the HIV/AIDS pandemic among youth in Nairobi. The letter outlined that the church would be responsible for the expenses of the trip. So, I applied for a B-1 visa, a temporary permit issued to individuals going for business or visiting. My application was scheduled, and on the day of my interview, the consular officer's first question:

"Have you applied for a visa before?"

"Yes, I have."

"Were you issued the visa?"

"No, Madam!"

"Why were you denied?"

"I was not given a reason why I was denied."

There was a moment of silence as she looked through my document. She looked into my eyes and said, "I am sorry, I cannot issue you a visa today. The reason for your denial is circled in this paper. You can read through it, and if your circumstances change, you can reapply." It stated, "Your visa application has been reviewed, and you do not currently qualify for a visa." Period! There was no further explanation of what could change my circumstances or what could make me qualify for a visa. I was extremely fed up with the US Embassy taking my money and not issuing me a visa.

This last denial for a visa raised thorny questions: Who goes and who stays? Who qualifies for a visa, and who decides who gets a pass? Who gets access to enter the United States, and who doesn't? The United States, throughout its history, has significantly benefitted from the arrival of new people who bring with them fresh energy, ideas, and ambition. Still, the system has yet to make it easy for immigrants coming to the US. After this denial, I decided to put on hold any attempt to apply for a visa interview and concentrate on going to Liberia to search for my family.

Later, after I got married and returned to Liberia in 2007, I decided again to give it a shot and applied for a visa to visit with my wife. I showed up to the interview with no expectations. My attitude was, "If they give me the visa, well and good; if not, I am at home and content." By this point, I'd developed a misanthropic view of the US embassy as a neocolonial institution extorting money from poor Africans to increase their wealth. Their actions and attitude toward visa seekers hoping to enter their country depicted certain remnant features and agents of the colonial era. I was cynical and furious and did not want to go for the interview. I remember my wife saying to me, "You are doing it for your family in the US so that they can get to meet you and you can meet them."

The consular officer interviewing me pulled my records from their system and, realizing that I had been denied access previously, asked me why I was denied a visa. I was forthright and said I was told I didn't have strong ties that would bring me back. "What has changed in your status since your last interview?" she asked.

"Well, I am back in my country of birth, working, married, and owning one and a half acres of land. I am established here; I am just going for a visit and coming back," I said. She looked at me and said, "You just returned home, gave yourself a few years of work, then reapplied." I was denied a visa, but I was not yelled at, nor was I humiliated. I left not feeling frustrated and angry. However, I was disappointed because I had invested time and money in the application process. I did not have any negative emotions because of denial. Instead, I was at peace, content with how the consular politely talked to me.

After that experience, we decided to take a different route: to apply for a marriage-based Green Card, and we began dealing with US Citizenship and Immigration Services (USCIS). Having had considerable experience with the US Embassy and multiple visa refusals, I went into it knowing it was not going to be easy. I concluded that visa issuing is a mystery that only consular officers understand. Is it a money-making scam? It is estimated that the US embassy in Nairobi collects millions (if not billions) of shillings every year in visa fees from thousands of applicants who were never granted visas, and, due to long processing times, many who had perfectly valid reasons to temporarily visit the US did not receive a visa until way after the reason for their visit no longer existed. To me, and many other Africans, this simply meant that Kenyans were effectively subsidizing the operating costs of the US consular service and we felt cheated out of our money. I had submitted four visa applications for very legitimate purposes, and went to four interviews, which cost me four hundred dollars—a very substantial amount in Africa, yet was denied each time with little or no explanation for the reason. I realized that the American Embassy in Kenya was definitely the place to go if you want to be treated poorly and unjustly.

Traveling to another country can be an amazing and rewarding experience, but the process of getting a visa is costly and almost a form of emotional torture. My cynicism led me to compare heaven and the US Embassy. That is, "How much easier is it to go to heaven than to go to the United States? All I have to do to go to heaven is believe and accept the redemptive work of the Son of God on my behalf and live faithfulness for Him and then die and go to heaven. But in order to go to the US, you must toil, tear, and sweat, and in the end, you still do not get the permit you need to enter."

The US embassy in Nairobi can seem like a mysterious, overly safe building filled with spineless people, but that couldn't be further from the truth. Still, if you let your mind wander, many questions will arise. Why are people so rude at embassies, particularly at the US embassy? The staff at the US embassy is known for being disrespectful to Africans seeking visas to enter the United States. Also, the team (from security to consular officials) are trained not to be overly empathetic and courteous, or it is a job that requires much coldness to execute.

Despite all its claims of being a nation that welcomes immigrants, a melting pot that embraces diversity, the United States government representatives overseas did not reflect that; instead, they humiliated and treated genuine visitors trying to enter the US with disrespect and subvert their humanity. I wonder how many US citizens who travel to Africa face the same challenges for visas to enter. Most people sit right in their homes and apply for visas, pay the fees, and mail their passports to the country's embassy for their travel visas. No interview, and they are never told to demonstrate that they will return to their country of origin. Why must African travelers to Western countries, especially America, be scrutinized and made to swear that they will not stay? It seems to imply that those from African countries are all criminals seeking to permanently move to another country, even if it is temporarily for school. When Europeans or Americans want to move to Africa, they don't apologize. They say it with pride and are issued the permit without hesitation. I've never been in a privileged position where I don't need a visa to enter another country.

To undertake this humongous task, we needed the experience and knowledge of a paralegal (immigration attorney) who understood the US Immigration system to help us get a marriage-based Green Card. Lisa's parents hired an immigration attorney to fill out and file all the appropriate petition documentation on my behalf. This process was not easy. It took countless emails and phone calls between Lisa's parents and the attorney and between us and Lisa's parents about what papers we needed to submit. Sometimes, the attorney would like to clarify an issue or the interpretation of a document obtained from Africa; it would require lengthy phone calls to explain why the document was the way it was.

Occasionally, we would present a document that would be rejected because it was not the specific document needed, and we'd have to submit new evidence. This meant the process would be paused until the new evidence was provided. The process cost thousands of dollars, which included the attorney fees and all the costs of filing each form. To my approximation, the paperwork took over two and a half years from when all the papers were submitted and approved to when I got the provisional green card.

Another example was sometime later, when Lisa and I traveled from Africa to the US, and we had a nine-hour layover at Heathrow Airport. We wanted to go into London, but because I was holding a Liberian passport and needed a visa to enter the UK, we could not go. In some instances, I was pulled aside at European immigration checks, asked questions, and sometimes taken to a room for interrogation, while my wife was standing on the other side waiting for me, simply because of the type of passport I held, the color of my skin, and my country of origin. Visa discrimination appears to be very racist and limits human development. Discrimination is a negative behavior, action, or practice that excludes or differentiates between individuals based on ascribed traits and that was how I felt whenever I sought to get a visa to the US.

Finally, in May 2009, I received a communication from the US Embassy in Monrovia to come for an interview. It did not come as a surprise because we've been awaiting that communication from the Embassy. After all, the US Government has already approved my Green Card. The interview was more or less to confirm who I was and provide some evidence of our marriage. I presented a photograph of our wedding and was issued a visa in my passport, which read, "conditional resident status." In April 2009, I entered the US to begin the process of removing the conditional resident status to permanent status. Once again, this was not an easy process; it was filing multiple forms, background checking, and fingerprinting. My conditional resident status was removed, and I applied for permanent residency.

Why did I choose to talk about my visa experience? It is an integral part of my story, and I want my readers to know the struggle I endured at the US Embassy in trying to get a visa. I am not the only one denied a visa through the US Embassy; each person has a unique story. Each person's case is different, but what have I learned in my process? Here is my assessment. Firstly, regardless of how credible your case is for going, giving legitimate reasons for entering the US and not being an economic refugee does not guarantee you getting a visa. Secondly, Africa is poor and underdeveloped, and it has a lot of political instability, so it is assumed that people will enter the US and desire to stay, which gives rise to a large number of us being denied visas as a result. Thirdly, it will always be challenging to be persuasive on the issue of intent—since it is subjective when a consular officer presumes to know what a person is likely to do in the future if they enter the US. Lastly, each person has a unique story; each person's case is different, and as a result, some might get a visa, and some will be denied.

15
Not Equal in America: My Immigration Story

"No matter who you are or what you look like, how you started off, or how and who you love, America is a place where you can write your own destiny."

—President Barack Obama

The immigration system in the US has been a touchstone of the US political debate for decades, as policymakers have weighed economic, security, and humanitarian concerns, making the USCIS scrutinize applicants and tighten the process to deter people from entering the United States. The immigration debate is ongoing, and Congress has not agreed on comprehensive immigration reform for years. As I narrate my personal experience, I want to do so to illuminate the challenges immigrants face when they move to America with the hope that it will serve as an encouragement for the many people like me coming to America for a better life. I hope to highlight the following challenges I experienced on my journey and perhaps provide a few valuable tips for overcoming each of these challenges and optimism to those who are in the process of their journey.

Culture shock, language barriers, legal and bureaucratic hurdles, financial difficulties, difficulty in accessing education and other resources, and homesickness. My story is similar to most immigrants who come to the United States, regardless of how we entered the US. It is essential to be aware of these common obstacles. The process of obtaining a marriage-based Green Card involves several steps. It is not a shortcut or easy way by any means! I am not an immigration expert, nor do I claim to know everything about US immigration policy. What I wish to share is purely based on my journey, and I will attempt to recap the steps I took in obtaining my green card.

Statistics do not tell the story of immigration. People do. Every one of us, as immigrants, has various reasons for immigrating. Some are fleeing war and violence; others are motivated by economic hardships and access to education and a better quality of life for future generations. By the same token, we all have divergent experiences and processes dealing with the system. The immigration journey, I must say, is a complex and challenging process. To obtain a marriage green card, I had to follow these steps:

Step 1: We had to establish the validity of the marriage relationship by submitting Form I-130 to confirm that my marriage to my American wife was valid, or bona fide. I had to complete the form and provide all the supporting documents. First of all, my petitioner—my wife, had to prove she was an American seeking a green card for her husband by giving documentation of her citizenship, including her birth certificate, a copy of her passport, bank account, showing the valid marriage certificate with our names, and the date and the place of the wedding. Also required were pictures of us together, showing proof that the marriage was not fraudulent, a joint bank account statement, proof that if there were previous marriages they were wholly terminated, and of course, her address in the United States. It is important to note that every step in this process required money.

Step 2: Once all the documents presented on my behalf were verified and approved, my petitioners, being my wife and her family, then had to file a Form I- 485, the primary purpose being to establish that I was eligible for a green card. This step was the adjustment of my status from being married to becoming an immigrant, and it had its critical elements, including the proof from my wife that she was financially stable and capable of supporting me in the US. She had to provide an affidavit of support and evidence of her tax returns. Then there was proof of nationality for me, which included a birth certificate and a passport photo page, as well as submitting filing fees and paying attorney fees totaling several thousand dollars.

Also required was a medical examination performed by a USCIS-approved doctor, and finally, a police clearance or background check record from every country I had lived in. For this particular document, I had to travel to Ghana and Kenya to obtain a background check, as well as one from Liberia. Securing these documents was a challenge as I was no longer a resident in those countries. I had to fly to each of them for a few weeks to process the background check. The wait time in this process was approximately one and a half to two years from submission to when USCIS processed it. As you can see, an immigrant like me, whose first language is not English and who does not know the system, faces extreme challenges in applying on their own, unless they acquire the services of an immigration attorney, which also requires a considerable amount of money. As a result, many immigrants are left shipwrecked and eventually become 'undocumented' immigrants.

Step 3: The final stage in the marriage-based green card process is attending an interview and awaiting approval. Once all of my documentation was received by the USCIS and reviewed, which probably took two years, I was invited to the US Embassy in Monrovia for an interview. This interview process was different than your typical visa interview session in that it was basically for the consular officer to assess the authenticity of the marriage. As I prepared for this interview, I was to remember every piece of information we had presented to USCIS on my behalf for a green card because the interview questions would primarily focus on our relationship history. The paralegal, Veronica Dejoie, whom my father-in-law hired, coached me. She tried to explain the techniques of responding to questions, having eye contact, and taking any physical evidence I might have that could show that I was married to Lisa. I took our big wedding photo album with me on the interview day.

Every question I was asked focused on our marriage, such as "What's your spouse's full name? How did you meet? Where did you get married, and on what date? Do you have any photos of your wedding?" I presented one of the wedding pictures that had us together with Lisa's parents, and I was asked to name those in the picture with us. The consular officer also requested another photo, and I presented one we took with some of our friends who attended the wedding, and I was asked who they were. When she was sufficiently convinced that the marriage was not fraudulent, she gave a date to go back and get my visa. When the date arrived, I went to the embassy. I got my passport with a visa stamped for six-month probationary period, was given a sealed yellow envelope, and was told not to open it until I arrived at my port of entry, where I would present it to an immigration officer.

In April 2009, I arrived on United States soil at John F. Kennedy Airport, entered a room full of other travelers, and presented the yellow envelope to immigration. I sat in the office waiting as they called each person individually to the window for verification. By this time, Lisa had picked up all of our suitcases, taken them to the other side of customs, and was waiting for me. It took so long that she got worried and wondered what the problem was. I was finally verified, my passport was stamped, and I was told, "Welcome to the United States."

Although I had the documentation to enter the US, it did not guarantee any privilege because I was on a *probational* green card, and we needed to prove that we were still living together. The immigration attorney that my father-in-law had hired to help file all the paperwork while we were in Liberia, was asked to work with us again as we tried to prove to the USCIS that we were still married and living together. This process required filing and submitting several legal supporting documents proving we lived together in the US. Furthermore, part of this application was to remove me from probational status and allow me to obtain an actual green card. Once all my documentation was verified and approved, I received a letter removing my probational status. I was issued an actual ID stating that I was a lawful permanent resident, meeting the 'continuous residence and physical presence' requirements in the US. This was before applying for naturalization, which was also a long and daunting task requiring paperwork and following more procedures and processes. My ID allowed me to gain employment as I waited for the next step.

After meeting the requirements to become a US citizen, including being a lawful permanent resident of the United States, physically present in the United States for at least five years, able to understand and speak English, and being of good moral character, my petitioner then applied for naturalization, through the form known as the

N-400. As part of the process, I was required to undergo a biometrics background check, fingerprinting, and provide proof that I was still married to my wife by giving a receipt of a significant purchase we both made together such as a car or household furniture, plus a picture of us and any pets we had.

Naturalization in the United States requires a thorough understanding of the steps involved. I remember my father-in-law taking me to an immigration attorney for a consultation and paying a fee of $2,000 for a couple of hours of asking questions relating to the law and what I should be doing to prepare for the interview and testing. At that moment, I realized how complex the immigration process can be, and that you don't want to mess up any step along the way. It also dawned on me that relocating to a new country can be a disorienting experience. It would be best if you had social and emotional support. I was fortunate to have a support system to help me in every aspect of the process, including financial support. We, as immigrants, often find ourselves in a new place where the rules have changed, the surroundings are unfamiliar, and the inhabitants speak in unfamiliar tongues. As such, we rely on people with compassionate hearts willing to support immigrants.

I finally sat for my naturalization interview and test and passed. I was so happy and excited that this chapter had ended. At the ceremony, along with other new citizens, I took the Oath of Allegiance. The judge swore us in and told us that 800 people had become US citizens that day. After that, the judge told us to go to the desk for our certificate of naturalization and that we had to give up our green card to receive it. I traded my green card for my certificate of naturalization. It was emotional to finally become a citizen of a country. My journey of being stateless and without a government was finally over. The small white paper, Form I-94, gave me the ticket to enter the

US, my green card helped me get my naturalization certificate, and my naturalization certificate recognized me as a US citizen. What a journey! I am grateful to so many people who played a role, especially my family, Gary and Carolyn Baughman, my wife Lisa, and the attorney who helped fill out every application correctly.

Despite these challenges, we immigrants have overcome these obstacles and built successful and fulfilling lives in our new environment. We, as immigrants, cannot narrate our experiences living in America without sharing our first impressions and culture shock. The following were my culture shock experiences upon arrival to the US.

Culture shock

"Culture shock" is a term that describes the disorientation and feelings of anxiety, confusion, and uncertainty that individuals experience when they encounter unfamiliar cultural norms, values, and behaviors. Moving to America was an exciting adventure for me, but it was a challenging and overwhelming experience, especially when adapting to the cultural differences in my new country. I remember my first day in America like it was yesterday. The large arrival area at JFK airport, filled with people worldwide, looked intimidating! There were strangers around me, each speaking another language, making me feel like I was in a dream. A security dog was sniffing my suitcases for contraband.

Moving from one culture to another is exciting. Still, it's also a very stressful experience. Transitioning from your culture, from everything familiar to completely new cultural stimuli, will always result in a culture shock. For me, America was this blessed land of plenty, a place of unparalleled opportunity, where the limit was only my imagination or my willingness to work hard. But moving to America, I had a big culture shock and my fair share of surprises. The following is the top of my list of culture shocks I experienced as an African immigrant.

The 'Fake' American Smile

Americans have huge smiles on their faces; did you ever notice that? At first, I thought they smiled because they were happy. And why wouldn't they be? Compared to where I came from, they lived in paradise. But then I realized that they don't smile only when they are happy. They smile all the time, as if they are plugged in. It took me awhile to realize that an American smile has little to do with emotions and a lot to do with being polite. But in recent years, it has become more apparent to me that there also exists much hate in America based on assumptions about skin color, sexuality, etc. Maybe people feel the need to smile politely when they are caught looking at you because they don't want you to think they are judging you, not open and accepting, or that they are a loving person who is just noticing their surroundings. This might especially be true when someone looks at me and my wife as a biracial couple.

The Sense of Personal Space

Americans do not like their personal space invaded. They find it uncomfortable when others stand too close to them and will unconsciously move away. Where I come from, there *is* no personal space. We are constantly near to each other. Americans don't like personal questions and consider it very rude if they are asked about their age, weight, or salary. You will hear a statement like, "It's none of your business." They also don't like to express their emotions. America was built on self-reliance and individualism—the idea that one should only rely on oneself and family to succeed. Therefore, they generally avoid getting too close to others. Whereas for us in Africa, there is a saying: "I am because we are, and since we are, therefore I am." This statement embraces the idea that humans cannot live in isolation; we live in a community and live life together and share whatever little we have with each other.

The "How Are You?"

Perhaps my biggest culture shock in America was the colloquial "How are you?" It took me a long time to realize that when the Americans say "How are you?" they are not actually asking how you are. It doesn't imply they are interested in your personal life. "How are you?" is just a greeting phrase that stops right there. So, the conversation goes something like this: *How are you? Good, and you? Pretty good! That's good.* This style of greeting was confusing for me. Back in Liberia, when somebody asks you how you are, they are genuinely interested in knowing if you are well or have some issue you want to share. And you take time to respond and share how you are and your challenges.

The Shocking Politeness

Americans are shockingly polite: they will hold the door open for those walking behind them, wait patiently in line, excuse themselves for being late or for bumping into you accidentally. They don't scream, they don't yell, and they don't gesticulate. Coming from a culture where people argue and talk loudly in a casual conversation, signal to get someone's attention, and cut queues to get ahead, this was a real culture shock!

The Informality

Informality is a uniquely American value. For me, it was one of the positive cultural shocks in America. Calling your elders, teachers, and superiors by their first names was unheard of in Liberia, and it still is in most cultures I know in Africa. But the most shocking thing was that American informality doesn't diminish people's respect for others. Calling someone by their first name is usually a sign of friendliness or acceptance, not a way to make one feel unimportant.

The Respect for the Rule of Law

Americans take the rule of law very seriously and are overcautious about what they do or say. Coming from a culture where the rule of law is written on paper and not enforced, one can bribe their way into anything. Don't get me wrong, I am not saying we didn't obey the rule of law—the rules were simply not always enforced as they should be. One of my biggest culture shocks in America was discovering how easily you can be sued in this country over nothing. I volunteered at an organization that works with lower-income families in an apartment complex and the organization rented one of the apartments for office space. The children could come after school to get homework help and be served meals. One day, I was there with one of those who had come early, and my boss warned me never to be alone with any kids in the office because they could accuse me of abusing them or implicate me and take legal action against me.

If there is a lawsuit to be filed, someone will file it. When I first saw TV commercials encouraging people to sue their doctors for bad outcomes, which often happens despite the doctors' best and most competent efforts, I couldn't believe my ears. No wonder physicians and nurses in this country spend more time documenting their procedures than treating the patients themselves!

I must confess that I still have difficulty getting used to some of these things. And yet, the effect of my culture shock in America shaped me well. It increased my self-confidence and creativity and helped me identify the many different types of people and their values. And most importantly, it helped me become more accepting and understanding toward other people. I realize that our differences don't define us and shouldn't divide us. There will always be contrasts between cultures, but they shouldn't affect people's relationships.

The Language Barriers

I was fluent in English when I came to the States, but little did I know that the same word can mean two very different things, depending on what side of the Atlantic you are on. One day at my workplace, in the breakroom, I asked a colleague for a pencil with rubber, and in an instant, everybody in the room looked at each other and burst into laughter. The innocent pencil eraser, the "rubber" as the British call it, is a condom in America. At another time, I asked the baker for a couple of buns at a bakery near our apartment complex. The lady behind the counter smiled and handed me the two cakes I was pointing at but said softly: "Honey, these are called rolls here. Buns are the ones you sit on." (Meaning buttocks).

Although I was fluent in English before coming to the US, I still faced a language barrier. It was difficult for people to understand me when I spoke because an accent accompanied my English. This made me fear speaking, and I felt isolated, hopeless, and anti-social, sometimes leading to depression. It made me feel like I was not a college graduate. Struggling with speaking and comprehension made it difficult for me to make friends. I felt like a target of laughter, causing me to lose confidence and inhibiting me from speaking and participating in social activities.

Many immigrants in the United States, like me, face similar barriers. The language barrier is one of the biggest problems people face when they move to another country. Many immigrants from other countries face many linguistic challenges that impede their control of daily life tasks and their ability to survive. Communication is an essential part of our day-to-day lives. We use it in almost everything we do. Although effective communication does not guarantee success for immigrants, its absence usually assures problems. In the US, language barriers can create many issues for non-English speaking immigrants like me, including but not limited to, difficulty filing immigration documents, finding employment, obtaining medical care, achieving education, and dealing with legal matters. As immigrants, we must force ourselves to speak the national language of our new country. If we cannot speak the national language, we cannot function fully and therefore become isolated and disempowered from the community. We must endeavor to speak the national language because it allows us to communicate, access information, and make informed decisions. As Garrett put it, "Language barriers are fundamental obstacles for immigrants. They hinder migrants from making vital connections within their communities and even to get around on a daily basis" (Peter Garrett, 2010)[13]

Legal and Bureaucratic Hurdles

As immigrants, we must deal with legal and bureaucratic impediments to the system. The US Citizenship and Immigration Service (USCIS), responsible for processing applications for immigrants, delays the process and holds sway over many people's lives. From my experience, it is evident that the process is complicated and confusing. When I applied for the removal of the probational status, I received a reply in two months that my application was received and was in process; but the processing period lasted one year. At the end of that year, I received another letter requesting additional supporting documents for my case. My life was in a holding pattern for years because I was waiting for a decision on my application to adjust my status to allow me to acquire a social security card and subsequently gain employment. Worse, it was impossible to inquire about the status of the application, and all I could do was wait until I got a reply. So, you need a support system to help you navigate the process from start to finish to succeed. Also, you need to read and understand the immigration processes to know the requirements and available resources. Finally, irrespective of the broken immigration system, do not engage in unlawful activities that might endanger your process.

Financial Difficulties

One obstruction for immigrants in the immigration process is the lack of financial resources to meet the cost of the process. When immigrants first come to America, they likely won't have a bank account. Without a job, you cannot have a bank account, and without a bank account, you can't pay bills and pay for purchases. Almost every aspect of your life in America requires money. As a newcomer in America, we faced financial difficulties, making it hard to find a trustworthy immigration lawyer to plead our case or even be able to pay for education. What could we do with our limited financial resources? My advice is that you live within your means and ask for help. There are resources in educational institutions and community organizations to support various needs.

Difficulty Accessing Education

Navigating the American educational system can overwhelm anyone, especially immigrants and their children. Immigrants face a variety of barriers when it comes to accessing education in the United States. These barriers include linguistic, cultural, and financial challenges, discrimination, and lack of access to resources. When I was trying to go to school here, my academic credentials from Africa were not being accepted. In other schools, I was asked to send my transcripts to an evaluating institution selected by the school to evaluate my academic grades to determine if I was of the required level as a graduate student. In addition, I was also required to write an essay demonstrating how I had matured since graduating from college and expressing my readiness for a graduate course at a US university. I was taken aback when asked to do this; but otherwise, I would not get access to education. It was obvious to me that discrimination and bias were significant barriers for immigrants in the education system, and sometimes negative stereotyping from school administrators that education in Africa was of a low standard. Moreover, as immigrants, we tend to have limited financial resources, which can also make it difficult to afford the cost of education.

Homesickness

Homesickness is "the distress or impairment caused by an actual or anticipated separation." (Thurber and Walton, 2012.)[14] As stated by Thurber and Walton, homesickness is a critical issue for people who have left their homes and their familiar environment and settled in a new country. Being displaced and living in a refugee camp in another country for several years gave me the insight to know that homesickness is a challenge migrants face in their new country. Even though technology has done much to bridge the gap across the miles, it doesn't eliminate homesickness.

Being an immigrant causes a sense of loss and grief. When I arrived in the US, specifically in Colorado, I did not know anyone except my wife and her family. I spent some of my time at home with the family and some time alone. When I was alone, I felt more deeply the loss in terms of family, friends, and environmental familiarity. I grieved for my country as a geographical space and a sociocultural and linguistic entity that signified belongingness. The sadness I felt when I arrived in the US made me miss my parents and our good times, and this grieving for the loss would make me irritated for no reason. I thank my wife, who was supportive, compassionate, understanding, and gracious with me during those difficult moments. She was always very intuitive and knew I was struggling with living in America.

I was unsettled in the early period following my arrival, due to disorientation, leading to tears, fear, and sometimes just frowning. All immigrants will acknowledge going through some form of homesickness, despite the apparent joy of having the opportunity to be in a land that gives them the privilege of achieving their dream. Homesickness can cause psychological and social disruption in our lives as immigrants. How did I bridge the gap between Home and Away?

I employed two strategies or paradigms to help me deal with my homesickness. First, I tried to develop and maintain my social networks with people from my home country and other countries. Once I started connecting with people, especially in my new country, I rapidly began to make sense of my hosts' realities and learned about their cultures. Secondly, I purposefully decided to maintain both local and distant connections. I did this by making phone calls back home, and I developed a personal willingness and drive to remain in contact with my host friends regardless of their busyness. As a result, this decision provided cultural immersion, a sense of self-worth, and cultural exploration and discovery. So, if you are an immigrant like me, I encourage you to experiment with these mitigating factors in your journey.

Many Americans oppose immigration and have negative views of immigrants because they have forgotten what it means to be an immigrant in the United States. Immigrants leave their home countries to chase the opportunities that citizens of America were searching for when their families immigrated many years ago. Education, work, and a better life for loved ones are reasons for immigration shared by immigrants today as well as those who arrived in the United States decades ago. People opposing immigration tend to maintain beliefs that are not necessarily true, such as the idea that immigrants take jobs or produce an increase in crime. The fears and concerns of the American people can be overcome with a greater understanding of immigrants and each other. Once we realize that we all come from the same beginnings, and that all of our families are made up of the same immigrants that many people hold so much fear towards, we will be able to move past our differences and toward a more understanding and more accepting idea of what it means to be an American. American culture is becoming unavoidably more linked with immigration as people continue to immigrate.

Being American isn't always the dream. I have been discriminated against for as long as I can remember, not only because of being an immigrant but also because I am a person of color. Whether it was a pastor telling me "I cannot give you a job because you don't have an American education," or being talked to a certain way, looked at, or yelled at, and it happens without failure wherever I go. Being American means that you must face the reality of discrimination and adapt to it. If you have not yet experienced living here as an immigrant, I can guarantee you that at some point in your journey, you will encounter discrimination and racism. But don't give up on your dream regardless of the obstacles.

16
Sacrifice for Africa: Call to Return

"Great achievement is usually born of great sacrifice, and is never the result of selfishness"

—Napoleon Hill

When Lisa and I married and moved to the US, we immediately started reimagining our future and discussing our return to Africa. Central to our discussion was what we wanted to do when we returned to Africa and where we wanted to go. Why were we so passionate and determined to go to Africa, a continent ravaged by war, corruption, terror, genocide, and disease? Steve Jobs once said, “People with passion can change the world.”

My wife is a social worker, and she loves what she does and does it passionately. She taught me that the only way to do great work is to love what you do. Lisa and I met in Africa, fell in love with each other, fell in love with the people of Africa, and served alongside them. It had always been our hearts’ desire to one day live and work somewhere in Africa. Africa is a continent that captures the attention of all the world, and once it has possessed us, we never wanted to leave. In Africa, the fastidious can become cavalier about dirt; racists can jettison bigotry; and fears can wash off like dust after a rain. In retrospect, I know that study-abroad students often say they no longer recognize themselves upon their return to the US, and they sometimes claim they have become better and learned something about themselves and life that they wouldn't have learned elsewhere. At the end of their semester in Africa, students often answer the question of how their experience changed them with responses such as:

"My host family showed me how to be a great hostess. The warmth and generosity I felt was unlike anything I've ever experienced. They took me under their wings, and honestly, I've never felt more welcome in a new environment than I did there. They are hospitable and giving."

"I learned so much about myself. That sounds so cliché, but it's the absolute truth. I've never lived overseas for an extended period, and I found myself immersed in an unfamiliar culture. Instead of sinking, I chose to swim. I tried new foods, drank new drinks, talked to people I normally wouldn't have, and learned to sit back and observe. I learned that I am strong."

"I have a different perspective on Africa. Let's be honest, the media doesn't portray the African continent in the best light. But truth be told, Uganda had a vibrant city center, booming with new construction, and will probably be a hub for big business in Africa within the next ten years."

Every year, after their studies, many returned to explore and learn more, and some continued to live and work in Africa. Like those students, we, too, wanted to return and follow our passion to serve. I've always had a passion for helping others, and I love the idea of being considered a dependable person. I enjoy when others come to me to talk about the hardships they are experiencing and I am able to provide them with feedback or helpful advice. To do this, I learned I needed to have the characteristics of a "people person."

The more we talked about returning to Africa, the more I realized that acquiring an education in the healthcare profession would help prepare and equip me to serve well in Africa. I was drawn to the health profession because it was one of Liberia's significant challenges when Lisa and I worked there. In the aftermath of the 14 years of conflict, people's health and their ability to survive were fragile. During our time in Liberia, due to the country's shortage of healthcare personnel, we constantly responded to urgent medical needs in addition to our emergency relief and development aid work with Samaritan's Purse. Most of our health-related work was either transporting sick people to a distant healthcare facility or providing community health education in the community to prevent people from acquiring preventable diseases.

Recognizing this need in Liberia, and now living in the United States, I decided to take advantage of available resources to learn about community health education. In 2012, I applied to Colorado State University's online program (CSU-Global) to earn a master's degree in public health administration. I was accepted for the program and started classes, though I was also working at Target and was comfortable with what I was doing. However, midway into my first semester of the program, Lisa was informed by one of her friends about a career opportunity to work as a social work coordinator in a study-abroad program in Uganda under the auspices of the Council for Christian Colleges and Universities (CCCU). This would involve supervising undergraduate students studying for a semester at a Ugandan university. Lisa was excited about the prospect of returning to Africa and working with American college students alongside African professors at the university. She went on to apply for the position, was called for an interview in Washington, DC, and a couple of weeks later was offered the job. She accepted the position, meaning that we would be moving back to Africa!

Growing up in a society with limited opportunities to develop and flourish, the thought of returning to Africa so *quickly* made me question that decision. I was born there and lived there, so I knew what it takes for humans to flourish, and it takes much more than merely the absence of suffering. It is about enabling people to achieve their full potential and to live the lives that they value. But achieving this in Africa is a challenge for many reasons. The continent has lots of problems: ethnic conflicts, corruption, a poorly funded educational system, high rates of unemployment, and hunger. There is also famine, poverty, disease, and inequality. All of these things that inhibit people from flourishing can be found in Africa.

Given all of these issues, I was extremely hesitant to return immediately, having just arrived three years earlier in the United States to seek a better life. Besides, relocating overseas long-term is a big decision you must take seriously. The decision to leave familiar surroundings and adapt to another social and cultural environment should not be taken lightly, for when you travel or live abroad, you leave behind critical support systems. It can also be extremely challenging if the move is to a country that is not the home country of either you or your wife. Therefore, I struggled with the idea of returning to the unfamiliar country of Uganda, a country that neither of us had ever been to, and where the insurgency of Joseph Kony's "Lord's Resistance Army" was taking place. I had just escaped from a war, and the thought of going to a country that was potentially emerging into a similar conflict was terrifying.

However, I remained composed and continued to support Lisa in the process. I could not stand in the way of her not taking her dream job. After an introspection of what Lisa had experienced and endured in Liberia with me during our two years there, I felt accompanying her to Uganda and supporting her as she worked with students would not be *anything* compared to living in the "Bug House" in hot and humid Liberia. Additionally, Kony's Lord's Resistance Army was not anywhere near the location we were going to. Thus, after solemn prayers for calmness, peace, and conviction about the situation, we felt it was the right call to move to Uganda.

In May 2012, I quit my job at Target and said goodbye to my coworkers—right after I had been announced as the Employee of the Month in a team meeting! My supervisor was shocked that I was leaving, and she revealed that she was relying on me to go with her to work at a new location, Colorado Mills, where she would be the manager. I expressed my apology, we hugged, and she said goodbye. It was emotional for me to leave because I had become accustomed to the work environment at Target, and the people were friendly and welcoming compared to my first job in America as a mail handler at the United Parcel Service (UPS). The working hours there had been horrible, working from two a.m. to eight a.m. During that period, I'd had to sort hundreds, even thousands, of packages and carefully place them in the delivery van according to their delivery labels. It was my first fast-paced work environment in the US, and getting accustomed to the US work ethic was a big challenge, especially getting used to what was and wasn't acceptable at work. For example, making time to get to know the people you work with was unacceptable in the workplace. It was considered a waste of time. With my African mindset, relationships are more valued over work and sticking to a schedule for the day. It became clear to me that a work relationship could impair productivity. Therefore, my African mentality of building community in the workplace was rebuffed. I quickly discovered that Americans love keeping busy and productive because it makes them feel valuable. Since we live in a capitalistic society, we operate under the notion that workers' labor produces value. Therefore, we often feel disposable if we aren't proving our worth through hard work.

Moreover, I had a boss who was very racist, condescending, and never satisfied with my work. One day, while sorting and loading the delivery van, I placed a few packages in the wrong delivery slots, and the driver did not deliver them even though they were in his van. The next morning, after the motivational speech he usually gave before the start of the day, my boss called me aside to talk to me about my mistakes and how much that had cost the organization to correctly deliver that mail to the proper recipients.

From then on, I became the target of his supervision, checking out everything I did. He would use the scanner to verify if I had placed each package in the appropriate delivery slots in the truck—something he never did with my colleagues. This, of course, made me think that he was targeting me and did not trust me anymore. He would yell at me for every little mistake I made, sometimes using racial slurs directed at me. I complained to the HR Department and requested to be placed under a different supervisor, but the HR personnel were adamant that the supervisor was the only one responsible for the assignments. Immediately after leaving the HR office, I was ready to resign. I came home, wrote my resignation letter, and took it to work. After work that morning, I walked to the HR office, submitted my resignation letter, and walked out. I served in that organization for only two months.

Lisa and I began the daunting task of packing our suitcases, selling our stuff, and buying *new* stuff we thought might not be available in Uganda. Toward the end of May, we had two garage sales and then packed boxes of items we wanted to store while we were away. We put our car, 'Ruby,' up for sale on Facebook Marketplace and fortunately, we got a buyer, which was a massive relief because we needed that money to buy a car in Uganda. At the beginning of June, we invited all our friends and families to come and celebrate with us, and we used that occasion to say farewell.

After the farewell party, we still had a few things we needed to take care of, such as finding a home for our dog, 'Kola,' and storing the stuff we were leaving. Our friends and family were so kind and generous to allow us to store our things at their houses while we were away. Someone offered to keep our bedroom furniture, another agreed to keep all our kitchenware, and Lisa's parents took the rest of the stuff into their garage and basement. When everything was said and done in July, we left for Uganda.

We arrived in Uganda on a KLM flight and were met upon arrival at the airport by the director of the Uganda Studies Program (USP), Mr. Mark Bartels, who then drove us, along with a new program assistant, to Uganda Christian University in Mukono. We met Mark's wife, Abby, and their three kids. We met our neighbor, Rachel Robinson, one of the coordinators with whom we shared our apartment building. She lived downstairs and we occupied the upstairs rooms. Everyone was considerate and offered their services to help us settle in.

The students arrived a month after we got to campus and Lisa began her job as a social work coordinator. I stayed at home daily, helping to get settled, and occasionally Mark would invite me to accompany the program coordinators on trips, especially to Rwanda or the rural homestay sites with students. Those travels helped me understand the USP programs, and I got to know students. Mark also allowed me to teach an elective course called African Christian

Theology for two semesters on a part-time basis. Subsequently, I was employed to work with the program as the Host Family Coordinator, a position I held till October 2020.

In 2015, Mark and his family turned over the leadership of the USP to Rachel Robinson, and under her leadership the program continued to flourish, with many students being attracted to the program, as it did under the supervision of Mark. Rachel thus became our boss, but also a very close friend of our family. We shared life and had many moments of laughter, fun, and joy. Rachel has a beautiful heart and was always giving herself in the service of others. She is among the most selfless people I have ever worked with, and it was a joy to work with her and get to know her as a friend as well.

During our eight years in Uganda, I learned that opportunity often comes disguised as misfortune. I was hesitant to go to Uganda, but I had something to offer. My skillset was valued and utilized at Uganda Christian University, rather than in the United States where I was asked to write an essay to prove that I was qualified college material, even though I already had a master's degree. In some instances, I was denied a job due to discrimination; I looked and spoke differently with an accent. For example, I was offered a job, and later, the employer sent me an email to rescind my job offer based on having lived abroad for an extended period. I am unsure if a white American would be denied a job because they had lived abroad. Furthermore, going to Uganda helped me to reimagine myself as worthy of doing something worthwhile and impacting the lives of others. I was also privileged to teach conservative White American students who unabashedly thought that their culture was the "right way to live."

In 2018, I also started a nonprofit organization called the "Msingi Soccer Academy." Msingi's mission was (and still is) to create opportunities for underprivileged children and youth living in poverty by providing:

- Access to education
- Access to soccer skills development
- Access to healthcare
- Mentorship and culture change

Our program currently has 25+ youth involved, and ten of these are fully sponsored in primary and secondary schools. I am thankful for the many friends and families who continue to support the work of Msingi. While deciding to go to Uganda seemed like a loss, because I was leaving my job and abandoning my school and familiar environment, I actually gained much more than I expected. In Uganda, we adopted our son, Zeke, who has become the apple of our eyes. Going to Uganda was a blessing in disguise, and I will always be grateful for following my wife to Uganda.

17
My Experience with COVID-19

"This pandemic has magnified every existing inequality in our society—like systemic racism, gender inequality, and poverty."
—Melinda Gates

"Severe Acute Respiratory Syndrome Coronavirus 2 (SARS-CoV-2), also known as Coronavirus Disease 2019 (COVID-19), was discovered in Wuhan, China in late 2019. Although the virus resulted in variations in the severity of symptoms, the virus's infectious nature quickly grew into a global pandemic."[15]

Before the pandemic, my family and I had lived and worked in Uganda, coordinating a study abroad program for North American students. Then, in the Spring of 2020, the World Health Organization (WHO) declared the coronavirus, COVID-19, a global pandemic. As the disease rapidly spread in the West and China, and the WHO announced it as a global pandemic, Uganda was carefully watching and preparing for measures should the virus reach Africa and Uganda.

As the virus continued to impact many countries across the world, Uganda reported its first case of COVID-19 on March

21, 2020. It was reported that a businessman from Kampala, who had traveled to Dubai in the United Arab Emirates (UAE) prior to his return, presented a fever and flu-like symptoms at Entebbe International Airport. He tested positive for the virus and was quarantined. Consequently, individuals who had been to the UAE two weeks before the first case, were traced by the Ministry of Health and subjected to institutional quarantine. However, from then on, there was a rapid increase in the number of cases, most of which were cases imported from abroad, and the government took measures to identify and quarantine those individuals.

Our educational program at Uganda Christian University in Mukono had a crisis management plan outlining how to respond to critical situations that would negatively affect our ability to operate. That plan provided well-documented responses to potential crises and outlined possible action plans. However, in the case of the pandemic, the unusual need to limit transmission was beyond the scope of our crisis management protocol. Nevertheless, we were still discussing and considering possible actions to keep our students safe and get them out of the country.

I must admit that COVID-19 put our model of crisis management to the test. This was not just a typical crisis, but a *global* crisis requiring a *global* solution and we were at a loss as to what to do. Our routines and everyday habits were entirely shaken by the pandemic that had burst into our lives. While new social patterns were slowly forming here and there, there were significant differences depending on various situations regarding family, gender, occupation, and social position.

For our family with a small child, it was difficult to adjust our daily routines. While children appeared to experience milder symptoms from COVID-19 infection than older individuals, sudden changes in routines, resources, and relationships due to the restrictions on physical interaction significantly impacted families with young children. The children's social and support networks were broadly disrupted without school, childcare, extra-curricular activities, and family gatherings. Additional responsibilities for the parents further compounded the stress as they adapted and tried to balance their roles as educators and playmates with their stressful changes at work.

I had to teach my four-year-old son every day, creating lesson plans, playing, and participating in extra-curricular activities. Indeed, COVID-19 changed our lives as a family, including employment, financial stability, our son's education, our family's well-being, and our continued efforts to protect ourselves from contracting the virus through social distancing, sheltering in place, restricting travel, and implementing many challenging health protocols. It was very stressful for us being away from family support for childcare. Lisa and I cooperated and worked together on domestic chores, childcare, and teaching our son, which somewhat helped ease the stress level on each other.

Between March 21 and April 5, there was a rapid increase in the number of COVID-19 cases in Kampala and other parts of the country. The President declared a complete closure of primary and secondary schools and prohibited all gatherings in public places, thus limiting the number of people that could use public transportation. As the government tried to gain control of local transmission, borders with all the neighboring countries were closed. The authorities justified the lockdown measures as being intended to limit contamination and avoid deaths, but above all, to protect hospitals, as that part of the infrastructure was not sufficiently equipped to handle the crisis.

As the virus profoundly threatened the country, President Yoweri Museveni took another drastic step and closed all universities and imposed a complete lockdown, which meant no movement of people or vehicles, and all businesses were closed. On March 25, 2020, the government banned all public transport and non-food markets. Prior to that, it had closed all bars and instituted a mandatory quarantine in hotels for Ugandans returning from high-risk countries—for which those in quarantine initially had to pay. Several additional measures were taken, including a nighttime curfew, banning all privately owned vehicles, and closing shopping malls and food stores. The government also announced that police and the Army would conduct patrols to enforce the new directives. However, in many cases, these security forces used excessive force, including beatings and arbitrary detention of people. It was a difficult time, and in the face of all this, we were looking at a possible closure of the Uganda Studies Program.

A Zoom meeting was held, and all "non-essential" employees were laid off. I was then out of a job, and a week later, the senior management team of the Council for Christian Colleges and Universities (CCCU), including the President/CEO, had another meeting to communicate that they could no longer run any overseas study abroad programs due to the financial implications that COVID-19 had presented. This meant that the Uganda Studies Program, along with all other overseas programs of CCCU, were going to be discontinued. All this was happening amid a lockdown, and the organization was saying that it would no longer be responsible for its overseas staff. In effect, our employer had abandoned us with no consideration or discussion of how it could help its employees living abroad to leave and join their families at home. In addition, our safety and security were not even considered as a part of the discussion.

One can imagine the direct and indirect social, emotional, and financial impacts that this abandonment had on us, being stranded in a foreign country during a pandemic! Along with that were the international travel restrictions introduced by the Ugandan government in response to the pandemic, which prohibited us from leaving the country, even if we had the means to do so. In addition, most countries around the world had implemented international travel restrictions and had closed their borders to anyone coming in.

So, we had to remain in Uganda, on the Uganda Christian University campus, quarantined with our friends and coworkers. We built our little community, shared meals, took walks, and implemented other coping mechanisms. The campus was quiet, as most residents had gone to their up-country villages to escape the city's restrictions. We got food supplies left in our coworkers' fridges since we had access, who had managed to leave the country under a police escort to the airport arranged and paid for by them to board one of the US Embassy's organized flights. After being indoors for several weeks, on April 16, 2020, Rachel, Lisa, and I bravely walked into the nearby town of the university where we worked to see if we could get some groceries.

The city was utterly deserted, and very few people were in the grocery store. Social distancing, wearing masks, and washing hands were required before entering the store, and only a certain number of people could enter at a time to maintain the social distancing rules.

When the government finally started lifting restrictions on lockdowns, thus marking the start of a slow return to "normalcy," we were able to leave our house and travel outside of Kampala to a national park to rest, enjoy nature, and heal from the stress of lockdown restrictions. After four days at the park, we returned to Kampala to consider the possibility of leaving the country. In early October 2020, we received an email from the US Embassy (to American citizens living in Uganda) confirming the availability of a commercial flight, organized in coordination with the government of Uganda, for American citizens who desired to return home. We immediately applied, registered, and bought our tickets to leave.

18
Hit by Multiple Myeloma (MM), and the Patient is Me

"Cancer cannot cripple love; It cannot shatter hope; it cannot conquer the spirit."

—Unknown

Insights into my Disease

Prior to leaving Uganda in October 2020, I was living with my family, enjoying my work with the Uganda Studies Program on the Uganda Christian University campus. I was a very healthy young man, active, and heavily involved in various physical activities such as sports, jogging, weightlifting, and running a non-profit organization that I had founded. However, upon our arrival in the US in late October 2020, I started to experience pain in my lower back.

In December, I made an appointment to see my primary care physician (PCP) for an annual checkup. Blood was drawn and analyzed, and a week later when I returned to my PCP to discuss the blood work results, he told me that my protein level was elevated, and he requested another test. Immediately, I was alarmed and worried about what could be causing the elevated protein. The second test results also showed high protein levels and I was still experiencing back pain. At that time, he directed me to an oncologist for further assessment and suggested that I go to physical therapy (PT) with the hope that this might help resolve the pain in my lower back.

After two weeks of physical therapy, the pain was much greater, and I could barely walk. Based on all the test results, I was to be admitted to the Rocky Mountain Cancer Center at Saint Anthony Hospital in Lakewood, Colorado. They wheeled me upstairs, admitted me, and ran tests for five days, including a biopsy, an echocardiogram, and ultrasound. The results revealed that some of my internal organs were damaged, and the biopsy results showed multiple myeloma. It was the first time that I had ever heard the word.

"What's myeloma?" I asked Lisa, who was sitting next to me, rubbing my back to console me due to my anxiety and stress. We learned it was a malignant tumor of the bone marrow. She asked the oncologist what the way forward was and what were the treatment options.

The doctor responded, "We will start treatment immediately at Rocky Mountain Cancer Center."

Both of us started doing research on the internet to learn more about the disease. As I read, the information I got was not encouraging. I read that the disease had no cure, but research was ongoing to find a cure. and that there had been some breakthroughs with drugs to help patients with MM stay longer in remission. It is still tough to read some of the material when the first line starts by reminding me that there is no cure for MM. Other patient information was a little less dire and said that it's rarely curable (implying that it *can* be cured), or that only a few people have been cured. Well, maybe I could be one of those few people.

After five days of hospitalization to discover the cause of my pain and discomfort, I was discharged, and I started four months of grueling chemotherapy at RMCC. In the meantime, I had several consultations for possible radiotherapy options to help reduce my pain.

Worry and distress immediately took over my life. I had anxious thoughts swirling around in my head at all hours of the day and night. I was angry, sad, scared, powerless, and stunned. I am glad I had my lovely wife by my side, and even though we were heartbroken and confused when we were told the news, Lisa was attentive to what the oncologist was explaining, taking notes, and asking questions. She asked as many questions as she could to get all the necessary information as we embarked on this new path. We'd had our dose of pain together, but this new path was foreign.

Insights as a Patient

When I was diagnosed, I decided to go into this trusting God for His miracle and trusting my doctor to provide the proper healing treatment. I had little idea of the disease or treatment options, and I began going in regularly for treatment.

I went through five cycles (twenty-one days each) of induction therapy. I was started on VRd (or RVD) standard therapy with bortezomib (Velcade), lenalidomide (Revlimid), and dexamethasone. In addition to these three medications, I started valacyclovir, aspirin, and pantoprazole for varicella zoster virus reactivation prevention, deep vein thrombosis (DVT) prevention, and gastrointestinal protection, respectively. Lisa bought me a very colorful morning/evening pillbox into which we put all the medications I needed to take every day.

Thank God for Lisa, who helped determine those medications, at what time I should take them, and the pre-medication I needed to prevent the side effects. Of course, some side effects would crop up throughout the treatment cycles, but the doctor controlled and managed them. If I were to be asked which medication had been the most challenging in my treatment, I would choose either bortezomib or lenalidomide (Revlimid), mainly because they are my regimen's official chemotherapy medications and because I had the worst side effects from taking those medications. Taking those medications made me vomit profusely and weakened my body. Dexamethasone-induced insomnia was also problematic because it messed with my sleep. I usually fell asleep fairly quickly but then woke up in the middle of the night and couldn't fall back to sleep. Those steroids definitely "crashed" me hard some days and I struggled to find the desire to do anything other than stay in bed.

I am astounded at the resources available to patients. I knew many of these services existed, but receiving a tangible benefit from many people and organizations has been an enormous blessing. I am doing my best to take advantage of those resources! So far, I have used my access to financial resources to support my family and myself, my case social worker to navigate and find the appropriate resources for which I qualify, pastoral counseling from the hospital chaplain, and survivor peer counseling. And there are still more resources to access!

It's fascinating to learn the varied issues that hospital staff and everyone associated with patient care are working through to ensure that all patients have the best support and resources they need. Taking advantage of this resource has been one of the best things in coping with the disease.

One of the hardest things I have gone through as a patient is the waiting process. Waiting for lab results. Waiting for appointments. Waiting for treatment to start. Waiting for treatment to end. Waiting for the next phase to begin. Waiting for the next phase to end. Waiting to get back to normal. One thing I have learned is that the waiting will likely never end.

Once I received my diagnosis and began treatment, I settled into a somewhat comfortable routine with the twenty-one-day cycles. After the second cycle, they decided to repeat my M-spike "just to see the level of the myeloma," The result showed that the M-spike had significantly increased, meaning that the myeloma was rapidly spreading. The doctor had to shift gears, develop a new treatment plan, and prescribe more powerful chemotherapy drugs for me that could help control the myeloma.

Insights into People Surrounding Me

A life-threatening illness or disease certainly impacts the person receiving such news, but it also significantly affects all those surrounding the patient. Naturally, my immediate family (my wife Lisa and my son Zeke) have been, and continue to be, impacted significantly as a result of my cancer diagnosis. Zeke has been constantly moved from place to place, between family members and friends, so that Lisa could be with me for all of my treatments and appointments. Lisa had to negotiate with her employer, Uganda Christian University Partners/Uganda Studies Program to see if she could work part-time at home so that she could have time to be with me and be able to work, take care of household duties, and support our family. I could talk for days about how each person responded. Each one was unique, and each response was remarkable. Lisa has been my chief caregiver, managing the communication flow and filtering information for me, our friends, and family. She also educated herself as much as possible about MM and its treatments, investigated various financial options, secured medical insurance, schedules hospital visits, takes Zeke to school, is in charge of my medications, and asks friends and family members to take me for treatment, etc. Managing and coordinating all these tasks singlehandedly, and doing it so well, is a remarkable feat.

My extended family (mother and father in-law, brother-in-law, sister-in-law, and nephew) have all been impacted in one way or another due to my illness. They have had to alter their lives and schedules to support me/us. They have frequently driven long distances to visit me in the hospital, sent texts and emails, and called to let me know they were thinking of me and praying for me.

As expected, the reactions from friends, acquaintances, and colleagues have been varied. Sometimes, people don't say anything for fear of saying the "wrong" thing. This can lead to feelings of isolation and a sense of abandonment of the person with cancer. In other instances, despite their best intentions, people say things that might not be helpful. I fully recognize that my diagnosis has remarkably impacted the people around me.

Insights into Myself

The insights I've learned about myself impact all areas of my life, but I've also identified several specific things about myself over these past two and a half years. My current circumstances have not made me waver in my trust in the One who created me—it has *increased* my faith in God. When I was twelve years old, I placed my eternal hope in Jesus Christ, and while my faith in God has not wavered throughout my life, I can certainly say that it has been tested. But lest anyone think I'm just a bit too pious for my own good, I freely admit that I have questioned, "Why *now*?" Why, at age fifty, must I deal with multiple myeloma cancer? Why, at this point in my marriage and my son's life?

I don't have specific answers to those questions, but ultimately, I know that God is in control, and everything works in His timing, according to His perfect will. I am also aware that He did not promise me that I would be free from suffering. Suffering is a part of life, so I can have courage and peace to walk through that suffering as I trust Him who has already given me ultimate victory. Sometimes, we get this idea that if we only had more faith, or if we'd just prayed enough or in the right way, all our suffering would go away, our sickness would be healed, and we wouldn't struggle. But God never promised this. In fact, Jesus said that we will have suffering; we will have trouble. What He promises isn't freedom from suffering, but His presence and peace in the midst of it. We can have ultimate peace because He has already ultimately conquered the world. The reality is that we may not experience full healing this side of eternity, but we can still have peace that comes only from putting our full trust in Him, knowing that He is writing a good story that is bigger than our current struggles, that He has woven His breath through every moment of our lives, and that He is with us and loves us no matter what worries or anxieties may fill our minds. He is our good father! He is with us through our aches, and He wraps our worries in His abiding love. "I have told you this so that you may have peace in me. Here on earth, you will have many trials and sorrows. But take heart, because I have overcome the world." –John 16:33.

On the day we shared my diagnosis with a few close friends, we received an offer of a home-cooked meal delivered to our house that night. Upon hearing of my diagnosis, there was an outpouring of sympathy and support from many people. Some asked if there was anything they could do to help, some offered to help by accompanying me to my appointments, providing childcare, or running errands for us. Lisa went with me to every treatment and doctor visit, and I've come to realize that I am very fortunate to have people that deeply love and care for me. A week before my stem cell transplant, my friend Rachel Robinson and her parents drove from Montana to come and be with me and encourage me. She also organized other friends to buy a new laptop for me to take with me to the hospital. This allowed me to stream my favorite soccer channel to watch my team play. The fact that she remembered when my treatment was due, and came immediately to see me, touched me deeply and reminded me that people matter. The fact that all of those people could understand and visualize the process was helpful to me and allowed them to be more invested in what I was going through. As others have said, "This is not just *my* journey; it's a journey for everyone around me as well."

I am often asked how I am doing physically, spiritually, mentally, and emotionally. At the outset, I must say that the physical aspect of cancer would be the most challenging because my body was exhausted from the chemotherapy drugs and other symptoms. Yes, I was challenged physically.

Spiritually, I have peace about where I stand in this regard, so this has not been a challenge, but rather an area of comfort for me. I knew God was with me, which gave me hope, and knowing that so many were praying for me was encouraging.

Mentally, I don't feel much has changed in this area. I've been very alert and aware of all the treatment processes. However, one neurologist I consulted with prior to my CAR T-cell therapy told me that I would probably "go insane" after I received the infusion. His exact words were, "You will go insane, but it will not last long, and you will get better." After the T-cells were infused into my body, I had daily clinic visits for assessment and blood work. The assessment usually involved asking these questions: "Which hospital and city are you in?" "What month and year is it?" "Count backwards from 100 by tens," and finally, "Write this statement on a piece of paper: Our national bird is the bald eagle." All this was to check my mental alertness and brain function, and I did all these things without fail!

Emotionally, I was challenged. I can say that I did have some particularly "down days" and a roller-coaster ride for a week. I thank my wife for her support and comfort during those dark days, as she definitely helped get me through those times. But there were, and are, other times, the times I don't tend to share with others, when the tears are on the surface, when the thoughts swirl at night and I can't fall back to sleep, or when I start to think of all the "what-ifs"—those times are hard. But it's usually during those times I get the "random" text, visit, or call to check in on me and pray with me.

Someone in my church "Life Group" once sent me a message at the right time. While the message, the words, the Scripture verse, the book to read, or song lyrics are often perfect for the situation, it's most importantly the fact that someone cared enough to reach out and say, "I'm thinking of you." For all those people who have done that for me and do that for others in their lives, I don't think they will ever honestly know what an absolute blessing they are!

The Next Episode

As the treatments continued, one of the next tasks we had to deal with was finding a permanent place to live. After we first arrived from Uganda during the pandemic, we drove directly to Estes Park from the airport to quarantine for two weeks at Lisa's parents' cabin. We then moved to Rebekah and Darren's house in Fort Collins for another two weeks, and finally moved to Denver and lived with Lisa's parents for three months. It was a blessing to have a family to host us and help us transition from Uganda, but we realized that having a place of our own would be a good idea, especially with our active four-year-old son. During this time, the sewer system at Lisa's parents' house became plugged, the basement flooded with water, and we all had to evacuate the house in order to repair the sewer line and the damage in the basement.

Lisa's parents rented a hotel for a couple of days, and we needed a place to stay while we waited for the work to be completed. Lisa reached out to some of her former childhood friends, seeing if we could stay with them until the crisis was resolved. One of her friends, Sarah, and her husband, Doug, graciously offered their basement to us without cost. While there, once again, Lisa reached out to her friends, asking if they knew of an apartment we could rent. One of her friends quickly found a two-bedroom apartment, without cost, for six months! When I heard this, my jaw dropped! How could people be so generous and compassionate to us? From then on, I knew we would have people walking this journey with us, both physically and emotionally. After the six-month stay in that condo, we were fortunate to have Lisa's parents find a beautiful condo for us with a view of a lake and the foothills of the Rocky Mountains.

Fast forward to 2021. The year started with continued chemo at RMCC and contemplation about treatment options. As I continued to have pain, even though I was doing weekly chemotherapy, my health continued to deteriorate, so my oncologist at RMCC recommended that we consult with a blood cancer specialist at the Colorado Blood Cancer Institute (CBCI) in Denver. We visited, and met with Dr. Henning Schade, a blood cancer specialist. After reviewing my file and learning about my medical history, he ordered a series of tests, including ultrasound, an MRI, X-rays, a bone marrow biopsy, a PET scan, and 24-hour urine analysis. After careful examination of the results, he outlined the steps for moving forward.

After several months of chemotherapy, radiation therapy, and taking the latest myeloma treatment drugs and injections, the myeloma remained—my cancer was very aggressive. The doctor opted to proceed with a stem cell transplant in hopes that it would eventually do the job. We had a lengthy discussion with the doctor and the transplant coordinator nurse about the procedures, processes, side effects, and what to expect. Once we felt that our questions were answered and we understood the treatment plan, my cells were collected and sent to a lab for processing and regeneration. Once the cells were ready to be transplanted back into my body, I was admitted and given a powerful blast of chemo for several days. This made me very sick, and I felt awful.

After receiving the transplant and being stabilized, I was discharged to go home. I continued having regular doctor visits and blood tests to monitor how well the transplant worked against the myeloma. On one of my doctor visits, he said the transplant had a mixed response.

"What does that mean?" we asked.

He said, "It did not do exactly what we had hoped it would do, killing the myeloma cells. Your myeloma number is going up rapidly." I was heartbroken again to hear that news! I sat there quietly with no words to speak. The doctor put his hand on my shoulder to console me and said, "There are other options we can try. Don't worry. We will shift to another treatment to control the myeloma number."

Over the next several months, the new medication seemed to be working well, lowering the myeloma number and almost putting me in "remission," so to speak. I had only a once-a-month treatment plan, my overall well-being was excellent, and I was engaging in physical activities and hoping the treatment worked. In January 2023, I gained employment at an assisted living facility called Morning Star and worked there for three months, which was a good indicator that I was progressing toward recovery and hopeful that I was on the verge of remission.

Based on how well my health had improved, we asked the doctor if we could take a trip back to Uganda to pick up our belongings, sell our car, and say a proper goodbye to all our friends and colleagues. The doctor approved us for that needed trip. In June 2021, we left for Uganda, where we managed to sell our car and say proper goodbyes to those we had worked with in Uganda for eight years. Upon our return from Uganda, our entire family contracted the COVID-19 virus. My doctor prescribed the drug Paxlovid, as I was immune-compromised, and we all soon recovered.

A week before my usual once-a-month infusion in April 2023, I noticed something was not right in my body. My stomach was suddenly bloated, I had no appetite, and I was extremely exhausted from minor physical activity. I then started to experience shortness of breath, accompanied by intermittent stomach pain. I tried to ignore all the signs and symptoms and just continued my life.

Over time, these symptoms continued to worsen. On the day of my treatment, I told the doctor about the symptoms I had experienced the week before. An echocardiogram showed fluid around my heart (pericardial effusion), and the results of an ultrasound scan were delayed, so the doctor told me to go home and that he would call and let me know the outcome. The moment I got home, the doctor called, but I was in excruciating pain, so I gave the phone to Lisa to talk to the doctor. The doctor told Lisa that the ultrasound showed that my gallbladder was inflamed, and I needed to go to the ER to be admitted so the gallbladder could be removed. I packed a few clothes in my backpack as Lisa called her parents to come and watch Zeke, and Lisa drove me to the hospital. The next day, another echocardiogram showed more fluid had accumulated.

Moreover, it was also revealed that a mass was seen on my heart. This news of a tumor in my heart brought sorrow and heartbreak. I was seized with fear, worry, and anxiety when I heard the doctors discussing how cardiac tumors are sporadic, and because the heart is an essential organ, even benign tumors can be life-threatening. I was afraid, afraid of the unknown, and I was nervous about surgery! I was worried about whether I would make it through, and I had thoughts running through my head, such as: What if I did not have a chance to say goodbye to my son or family? My wife tried to calm me down, but the level of intensity with which my cardiologist explained the rareness of the tumor, and the fact that they did not at that time have a specialist to perform a biopsy on my heart, did not help ease my anxiety and fear.

Oncologists and cardiologists continued to deliberate and consult about what to do, as it was very rare for myeloma to cause a mass on the heart. I was hooked to an IV line, receiving antibiotics and pain medication to control the pain in my stomach. The gallbladder could not be removed because of the pericardial effusion, so the fluid needed to be drained. It was drained (1000 ml), and the liquid was taken to a laboratory for analysis.

The following day, I underwent surgery to remove my gallbladder. Right after the gallbladder was removed, another echocardiogram was done to see if there had been any fluid buildup around my heart. Indeed, more fluid had accumulated, raising concerns regarding a transfer to a heart specialist for an invasive biopsy in order to determine what kind of tumor it was. While the possible transfer was being discussed and transportation scheduled, one of the oncologists, who happened to be on call only on that day, read in my medical record that the fluid had been sent to a lab, and he reached out to determine what had been discovered from the fluid. It was found that plasmacytoma had been identified in the fluid, which indicated that the myeloma had caused the mass and that I did not need to be transferred for the invasive biopsy on my heart. What a relief to hear that news!

The next day, my oncologist came to my hospital room and immediately I felt some hope and comfort. I had found comfort in my doctor's advice: "There will be lots of stops and doors to go through. Focus on the next stop and the next door. That is it. We will get you to stabilize." However, the pericardial effusion still needed to be drained for the second time, which meant that I would still need to be transferred to another hospital for a particular procedure to drain the extra fluid. The cardiologist was very concerned about the rate at which the fluid was building up, as it could cause increased pressure on my heart thereby reducing its ability to pump blood.

It was finally decided that I had to be taken to Aurora Medical Center. I arrived on Thursday, and early Friday morning I was taken to surgery and had two incisions below my breastbone and an incision in the sac surrounding my heart. A catheter was then used to drain the fluid. I had the fluid drained on Friday and Saturday and the catheter was removed early Sunday morning, followed by another echocardiogram. Once no fluid was found, the doctor discharged me and transferred me back to Presbyterian Saint Luke's Medical Center, where I was given five days of twenty-four chemotherapy drugs with the hope that it would shrink the mass. At the end of the five days, a further test was conducted, and the results showed that the tumor had shriveled, and there was no additional fluid. Now I had to recover from all of the surgeries, and while it was a great relief, the myeloma was still in my bloodstream.

Because of how stubborn the myeloma had been, and because other treatments hadn't worked, I was now eligible for "CAR T-cell therapy." This type of treatment involves filtering the blood to remove T-cells, "re-engineering" them in a laboratory to identify and attack the cancer cells, and then re-infusing them into the body. The science behind this treatment is mind-blowing! I was grateful to be selected as one of the recipients of this "living drug." These cells would live and multiply in my bloodstream like a cancer-killing superpower, providing immunity against my cancer cells. Is it not mind-blowing to think of the science of it all? I must say that the CAR T-cell therapy is a complex process that is undertaken by a team of experts with extensive experience. The process took about a month, and the steps included:

- Collecting my own T-Cells: The blood is drawn through a tube in the neck that goes directly to the top of the heart. The blood flows through the tube into an apheresis machine, which removes the T-cells. The machine then returns the rest of the blood back into the body through a different tube. It is fascinating!

- Engineering the T-Cells: My collected cells were sent to a laboratory in Massachusetts, where scientists engineered the cells and kept them for several weeks in order for the CAR T-cells to multiply and grow before returning them back to the collection hospital to be infused.
- Infusing the CAR T-cells: Once the lab produced enough CAR T-cells, they were sent to the Colorado Blood Cancer Institute (CBCI) where I had previously been treated. The cells were infused on July 24, 2023. I was then monitored frequently for signs and symptoms for Cytokine Release Syndrome (CRS), other fatal or life-threatening reactions, and neurologic toxicities that could lead to seizures. I was monitored intensely for fourteen days, with gadgets placed on my arm to check for severe infections, and a temperature patch under my armpit to check my temperature. The data was transmitted to the laboratory that manufactured the new cells. I also took regular blood pressure readings and daily FaceTime calls with a nurse using a tablet that was provided.

My cancer journey has taught me valuable lessons and revealed that human experience is vast and varied, but a few things exist as universal experiences, such as suffering and pain. While the pains and problems vary from person to person, we all suffer. This fact leads to the common question: "Why does God allow suffering?" Given this constant part of life, the wise person should seek to understand heartaches and how to react to suffering when it arrives. One of the most common responses is bitterness, anger, and a deep resentment for the pain we all go through. That has been my experience as I've dealt with myeloma and my many other sufferings. While suffering can undoubtedly sow the seeds of bitterness and resentment, that is not how Christians should respond to it. Instead, we are called to see suffering as a part of life meant to dissatisfy us with the present fallen world and to instill in us a longing for eternity. To unpack this idea, I want to share the lessons I have learned on this journey for the past two and a half years.

First and Foremost

Suffering allows us to minister comfort to others who suffer.

One of the most rewarding reasons that suffering has value is experienced by those who can say with conviction, "I know how you feel. I've been in your shoes." Suffering prepares us to minister comfort to others who suffer. Feeling isolated is one of the most complex parts of suffering, as it can feel like you're alone in your pain, thus making it much worse. The comfort provided by those who have known the same pain is inexpressible. It feels like a warm blanket being draped around your soul. But for someone to say those powerful words, "I know just how you feel because I've been there," that person first had to walk through the same rugged valley.

My wife and I lost our first baby through a miscarriage while living overseas. It was the most horrible suffering we'd ever known as a young married couple. This experience has enabled me to weep with those who weep with the comforting tears of one who has experienced that profound and awful loss. It's a wound that I can say, by God's grace, has never fully healed so that I can genuinely empathize with others out of the genuine pain I still feel.

We were in church one day when our pastor, during his sermon, shared about a couple who had a miscarriage and requested prayer for them. Thinking about their pain and suffering, and reflecting on ours, caused me to cry during the entire church service. Talking about my loss puts me in touch with the unhealed part of the grief and loss that will always hurt until God takes me to heaven and hopefully helps me understand it better. We don't know if the child was a boy or a girl, but regardless of the sex, we have promised to cherish and love her dearly.

One of the most incredibly comforting things I have ever experienced is someone else's tears for us. So, when I say to someone who has also lost a child, "I hurt with you because I've lost a precious one too," my tears bring warmth and comfort in a way that someone who has never known that pain cannot offer. When Lisa and I talked to our family on the phone about the loss of our unborn child, one of the most powerful words of comfort I received when we were grieving our baby's loss were the words from my sister-in-law and brother-in-law. I remember Rebekah saying, "Your pain may not be about just you. It may well be about other people, preparing you to minister comfort and hope to someone in your future who will need what you can give them because of what you're going through." And Darren said, "All that you've experienced, going through civil war and living in a refugee camp, can be a source of encouragement to others. And if you are faithful to cling to God now, I promise He will use you greatly to comfort others later." Those words turned on the switch in my heart, showing me that my suffering and loss were not pointless.

This all played out recently when I had the opportunity to talk with a fellow cancer patient named Dick, who had been diagnosed with brain cancer and was worried that he would die soon. Hearing Dick's fear, I was concerned that I didn't have anything to say to him that would bring comfort and assure him of God's presence with him. Still, it suddenly occurred to me that what I appreciated the most when someone came to visit me in the hospital was not trying to say something or answer my questions about suffering, but that they were there and were trying to hear and understand how I was feeling. They were just listening without always feeling like they had to respond. So, I asked Dick if he was comfortable sharing his journey, and I was interested to hear.

It felt good to sit and listen without feeling like I had to respond. Sometimes a caring listener is what we cancer patients need most. Once I had listened to Dick's story and heard the anxiety and stress in his voice, it allowed me to share my journey in the hope that it would be a source of comfort and encouragement and provide common ground on which to build trust, and to bond. God gave me the wisdom to help him focus on what brought him good feelings, like walking, religion, and visitation from a friend. When I asked him what brought him good feelings, he responded, "Taking a walk around the lake and enjoying nature and the company of my caregiver." He was quick to point out that he had given up on God. He pointed out that a kid in his past made him give up on God. I supported his feelings and allowed him to be negative. Our minds are powerful and play a key role in how we experience life. Our quality of life can be determined not by our circumstances but by how we think of them. Mind and body are interconnected; they exist in a synchrony such that your mind can affect your body and vice versa. I have also discovered that my heart rate and blood pressure go up when I think about stressful things. In a nutshell, our thoughts can affect our body, and our body can affect our thoughts. I have a friend named Sandrine, who showed me how to practice the mind-body technique in my healing process, and it has been a wonderful tool to show to others, including Dick. And so, I felt comfortable being present and allowing him to share, and I never wanted to change the subject. Ultimately, he allowed me to pray for him and assure him that God had not left or given up on him. God still loves us despite our circumstances or what we have done in the past. God's love is limitless!

There are no limits to God's love and faithfulness to us. No matter what it is that we have done, God is higher. His love is more significant than anything in our lives. When you're in pain, your world narrows down to mere survival, and it's easy for others to judge you for not "following the rules" that apply to those whose lives aren't being swallowed by the pain monster. At least it has been like that for me since I started on this cancer treatment path. My world has been narrowed down to trying to heal and survive after multiple chemotherapies, biopsies, and four failed cancer treatments for myeloma, including a stem cell transplant. Leaving me to fall into the pit of self-pity and worry, forgetting to seek God's face for my healing and restoration.

As I've been on this journey as well as experiencing suffering as a refugee, I tend not to judge others experiencing suffering because I know what it means to be in that position. Not being judged is a great comfort to those who are hurting and have had their share of suffering that is very uniquely theirs. Those who suffer tend to have tender hearts toward others in pain. We can comfort others with the comfort that we have received from God (2 Cor. 1:4) because we have experienced the reality of the Holy Spirit being there for us, walking alongside us in our pain. Then we can turn around and walk alongside others in their pain, showing the compassion that our own suffering has produced in us.

Second

This journey has taught me to lean into the pain and fellowship with Christ and my Christian community.

Philippians 3:10 says, "I want to know Christ and the power of His resurrection and the fellowship of His sufferings, being conformed to Him in His death."

Suffering provides space in our lives for deep intimacy with the One who has great empathy for our pain. We join in fellowship with Him in pain and suffering, as well as connecting with our community, giving them access to participate in our suffering.

As an African, our societies have taught us to be strong in the face of pain and adversity and to hide our pain. If others knew of our pain, doubts, and weaknesses, they would think less of us, lose faith in us, and no longer trust our ability to be community leaders. Actually, the opposite is true, from my perspective. I am not saying that we should open our lives to everyone in times of pain. Often, as we are going through a difficult season in our life, and we need to limit the level of access the "crowds" have to us. We need space to heal. Simply saying, *"I am going through a turbulent time. Please pray for me as I process this experience or as I deal with this obstacle or turmoil"* is important. A small, trusted community willing to pray for you and support and encourage you on the path of pain and suffering is essential in dealing with your grief.

When life leaves us gasping for air, prayer is how we can grasp the steadying, sure hand of God, and hear His gentle voice, "You're going to make it." You are going to relive a story you desperately want to change. This path has helped me discover the real purpose of prayer. It is not about convincing God to do what I want, but about awakening to what God is already doing and aligning myself with God's revolutionary, redeeming, and renewing work in my life. God's love is limitless. There are no limits to God's love and faithfulness to you. No matter what it is, God is higher, His love is greater, and He uses every circumstance in our lives for our good. Romans 8:28 is a promise that rang true for me, as it has been true for Christians throughout history. The living Bible translation puts it this way: "And we know that all that happens to us is working for our good if we love God and are fitting into his plans." The promise of Romans 8:28 that God works for our good "in all things" is reassuring. God is working in "all things," including our mistakes, in every detail of our life. God will take even your errors and work them out for your good. He reigns. He is sovereign in everything, and he works for the good of those who love him. The cross demonstrates that just as God took the worst event in history and turned it into the best, he can take the worst things in your life and use them for good.

It means that no matter the circumstances, there are only two qualifiers for God to be working all things together for our good. First, He works for the good of those who love Him. If you love God, you can trust that he is working for your good. He loves you back; when we love people, we seek their welfare. This is astonishing! It gives me hope that he is working out everything in my current circumstances. Second, He works for "those who are called according to his purpose." Because following God entails submitting to His purpose, and He has called us for a purpose, which is to serve Him and be an expression of who He is to the fallen world.

Third

Suffering develops a humble dependence on God.

Suffering is excellent at teaching us to have a humble dependence on God—the only appropriate response to our Creator. God keeps teaching me this truth, but I learned it and then turned away from it when life seemed to be working well in my favor. Ever since the fall of Adam, we keep forgetting that God created us to depend on Him and not on ourselves. We keep wanting to go our own way, pretending that we are God. Suffering is powerfully able to get us back on track. Living amid a war in Liberia, where there was no food to eat or water to drink, when I and a group of close friends were stuck in our hiding place, all we could say was "God help us, rescue us, and protect us." Suffering brings a "one day at a time-ness" to our survival. We get to the point of saying, "Lord, I can only make it through today if You help me… if You take me through today… or the next hour… or the next few minutes."

Suffering has taught me the lesson of total, humble dependence on God. Lying on that hospital bed, hooked up to an IV pole and being infused with cancer drugs, was no exception. Sometimes we hurt so much we can't pray. We are forced to depend on the intercession of the Holy Spirit and the saints, needing them to go before the throne of God on our behalf. Instead of seeing one's inability to pray as a personal failure, we can rejoice that our perception of being needy corresponds to the truth that we *are* that needy. 2 Corinthians 1:9 tells us that hardships and sufferings happen "so that we might not rely on ourselves but on God, who raises the dead."

As painful as it is, suffering strips away the distractions of life. It forces us to face the fact that we cannot change other people and most situations. The fear accompanying suffering drives us to the Father, like a little kid burying his face in his daddy's leg. Recognizing our powerlessness is the key to experiencing real power because we must acknowledge our dependence on God before His power can flow into our hearts. The disciples experienced two different storms out on the lake. The Lord's purpose in both instances was to teach them to stop relying on their physical eyes and use their spiritual eyes. He wanted them to grow in trust and dependence on the Father. He allows us to experience storms for the same purpose: to learn to depend on God.

I love this paraphrase of Romans 8:28: "The Lord may not have planned that this should overtake me, but He has most certainly permitted it. Therefore, though it were an attack of an enemy, by the time it reaches me, it has the Lord's permission, and therefore all is well. He will make it work together with all life's experiences for good."

Fourth

Suffering serves as a tool for our development.

Nothing is so broken that God cannot use it. Although suffering is alien to His goal for humanity, God uses it as part of our development as people. Suppose I had not learned that in the past; I am learning it now in my present suffering and pain. Nothing forces a person to confront their true self like suffering. Suffering causes our focus to turn inward, to face those parts of ourselves we might otherwise ignore. God can use suffering to develop us into better people who love God and enjoy being with Him forever (Romans 5:3-5; James 1:2-4).

We all experience pain in life, whether emotional or physical pain. We must all walk the journey that God has for our lives, yet God promises a purpose in all pain. We can press on each day knowing that God loves us and wants to use the hurt and pain in this world to bring Him glory. I don't know what you are going through, but God knows and will intervene. Don't give up hope; God has much more for your life! Give yourself time to deal with your emotions about having cancer. You may want to spend that time with loved ones or need time for yourself to process. Here are some suggestions and questions to help you manage your cancer:

What are my treatment options?

What are the most common side effects of each treatment?

Where can I get more information about my type of cancer?

It's a good idea to write down the questions you want to ask and take the list to your doctor visits. It can also help to have a friend or family member there to listen, take notes, and support you. My wife was so good at writing down the questions we wanted to ask the doctor.

How to get support:

Relationships take on new importance when you're faced with cancer. Your family and friends can help support you. You may also want to look beyond those who are close to you.

- Reach out to your family and friends. Remember that the people around you want to support you, and asking for help isn't a sign of weakness.
- Tell others how they can help. Your friends and family want to help, but some may need assistance in figuring out what to do. It may help to make a list. For example, you might ask them to:
    - Run errands or pick up kids.
    - Deliver meals or groceries to your home.

    - Drive you to appointments.
    - Go to doctor visits with you and take notes.

We've been so blessed to be around our family, which has been so supportive and journeying with us and has taken on many of these roles.

- Look for help from other sources. My wife has been able to reach out to many of her friends for support and childcare. Other places to turn to for help include:

Spiritual or religious groups

These groups can provide comfort and help you find resources or other social support services. It has been good to belong to a small group of like-minded people who pray for me, encourage and nourish me with spiritual food when I am discouraged and disappointed, and redirect my attention to God.

A cancer support group

Cancer support groups offer support and practical advice. You can hear others talk about what it's like to live with cancer and how they're coping. Unfortunately, I did not interact very much with people living with cancer. A friend finally introduced me to a lady living with myeloma, and even though we have not met in person, we have had time to talk on the phone, share our journeys, and encourage one another.

Social groups

Social groups can help you meet new people, get involved in activities you enjoy, and help focus your attention on activities that comfort you, such as spending time outdoors. Try to maintain social contact with friends and family as much as possible. Your friends might assume you want to avoid being invited to social events, but let them know to keep asking you if that is your preference. I have friends that compete in bike races, and occasionally they invite my family to go and see their races and cheer them on, and it has been helpful for me to get away and do something therapeutic.

Meanwhile, let people know about your physical limitations. Most friends and family members will be happy to plan quiet activities like going to the movies or fixing lunch or dinner at your house. And feel free to cancel if you are physically or emotionally tired.

Your healthcare team

Your team should be supportive, but you also have to be open and honest with them about your fears and concerns. Your doctor can help you get the proper medical treatments, including counseling. My healthcare team at CBCI has been supportive, directing me to valuable resources.

You may be worried about how your cancer diagnosis will affect your family and friends. A cancer diagnosis causes complex feelings and lifestyle changes that can overwhelm you and the people you are close to. I was unaware of how my diagnosis would change our family dynamic and responsibilities. Lisa, my wife, has had to take on more responsibilities, such as driving, planning schedules, getting work to provide bread on the table for the family, cooking, house cleaning, and paying bills. Cancer and its treatment have left me tired or unable to perform my usual tasks, and Lisa has had to pick up those duties. These added responsibilities may become overwhelming.

Meanwhile, I have felt guilty or sad for not being able to help her. She has never complained or gotten frustrated and resentful for the added responsibilities. Also, being able to accept outside help from friends and family members, even though challenging, has been helpful.

How can cancer affect your children?

Being a parent with cancer presents unique challenges. This is true whether you your children are young or grown up. Communication is vital for children and parents alike. I have not been very good at communicating with my son about my cancer. We've talked about Daddy being sick and discussed the type of sickness Daddy has, but I don't know whether he understands all that I tried to explain about my condition since he is only six years old. It was hard for him when Daddy spent a whole month in the hospital and he was not allowed to come and visit. He asked Mom whether Daddy was coming back. I tried to protect him from fear and other complicated feelings, but I wanted to talk to him openly about my diagnosis and treatment. I try to be honest about what is happening. I explain complex words that he does not understand and their meaning:

- Tumor — A lump of stuff that is not supposed to be there and can make you sick or hurt.
- Cancer — Stuff in your body or blood that makes it stop working as it should and makes you sick.
- Chemotherapy — A type of medicine that helps get rid of tumors. Chemo's main job is to make your tumor disappear, but chemo is powerful and can make your hair fall out. That is why Daddy does not have hair. But when you are done, your hair grows back.
- Port or pic line — A button that gets medicine into your body to help that tumor go away.

As a caregiver, my wife has also tried to help Zeke understand that Daddy is sick as Zeke asks questions and voices his worries and fears. Despite all these challenges, we love him, and we are all going through this together. For instance, one morning we had to wake him up at 5:30 a.m. to get him ready to take him to his grandparent's house, because I needed to be at the hospital at 7:00 a.m. for my CAR T-cell collection. He was so cooperative, and he did not cry, whine or throw a fit. We had discussed it the day before, so he understood why he needed to go to Papa and Nana's that early morning. Another lesson I have learned on this journey is that cancer is a test of strength, patience, and compassion. You will not do everything perfectly, and that is okay! Your family and friends' support network is so much more important than you will ever know. You can do this, and you will. Feel free to reach out and ask for help.

Conclusion

"Never give up! There are always tough times, regardless of what you do in anything in life. Be able to push through those times and maintain your ultimate goal."

—Nathan Chen

This memoir is about my life experiences that highlight the struggles, the roadblocks, and challenges I have faced in my life, and how those challenges and situations have determined the way I think and act, and how they have molded my character and developed in me a compassionate attitude. Challenges are a part of everyday life. They make us stronger, and without them, life becomes meaningless because we have nothing to compare the good times to. These challenges come in many forms. It could be escaping a violent civil war, living in a confinement camp as a refugee without your parents, and battling a health crisis. For some, the challenge is racism, fitting into a social group or culture, unemployment, or living in a country that is governed by dictator. For others, it may be seeking immigration status, social inclusion, doing well at work, or dealing with mental health issues. Regardless of these challenges, facing up to it is vital.

Doing so will make you feel like you can take care of yourself and understand the value of what you now have.

My confidence in the face of hardship has always been driven by my ability to reject the negativity that would hold me back. It is hard not to see challenges as problems and obstacles, but I've learned to see them as *opportunities* throughout my journey and have developed a resilience against the obstacles and challenges that life throws at me. If we have a choice, we can seek to avoid challenges. However, despite one's best efforts to avoid them, challenges arise and threaten our journey and our success, but we must handle them with resiliency. Although complex, challenges do offer benefits:

1. Challenges Make You Stronger

To build physical strength, you must apply a bit of resistance to your muscles. Challenges produce resistance, which develops inner courage. As you face and deal with challenges, you become stronger and stronger. Challenges are a superb chance for growth. They encounter your resolve and your commitment to your goal, and they know that you mean business. And after you overcome them, you develop emotional and mental strength.

2. Challenges Keep You Humble and Compassionate

I learned throughout my life that challenges remind me that I am human; I can't grasp everything, foresee everything, escape with everything. I have limitations, I have weaknesses, and I make mistakes. The challenges also remind me that I am very fragile, I need the support of others, and I have to take one day at a time. The experience of having gone through pain and challenges can also help us to better relate and be more compassionate to others. Humble people see life as a school, recognizing that while none of us is perfect, we can, without negatively impacting our self-esteem, work on our limitations by being open to new ideas, advice, and criticism. This ability alone cultivates an awe-inspiring inner strength, a most powerful example of which was Gandhi, whose autobiography represents a journey of humility and self-dissection. He once famously said, "I claim to be a simple individual liable to err like any other fellow mortal. I own, however, that I have humility enough to confess my errors and to retrace my steps."[16] If Gandhi is an example of what a humble person can accomplish, then we all need to follow in his footsteps.

3. Challenges Amplify Your Achievement

When you have to overcome multiple challenges to reach your goal, you appreciate your achievement all the more; these challenges serve as amplifiers for your success. Certain accomplishments wouldn't feel as valuable if they were less challenging. There was a time in the refugee camp when the thoughts of success were trumped by survival. I always needed more food because there was never enough food in the refugee camp. I spent most of my young life doubting if I would live to see the next day in the refugee camp. Likewise, during the war in Liberia as I was trying to escape. Today, I have two master's degrees, a beautiful family, and am a founder of a non-profit organization serving underprivileged children in Uganda, helping them to fulfill their dreams and aspirations. The journey that began my life has stretched in an almost unfathomable direction, and God ordered my steps.

4. Challenges Call for Creativity

Challenges force you to tap into your creativity to devise ways to overcome them. Some of the best ideas are conceived when you're feeling the pains of a challenge. Without the challenge, you would never have thought about that creative solution. When I lost my scholarship at Daystar University, I was on the verge of being sent back to my home country, but then I came up with the idea of selling cookies. When students wanted to study through the night, they liked to have tea and sometimes they wanted doughnuts or something to eat with their tea. So, they would come and buy biscuits. Although my earnings from the biscuit venture were not enough to pay my tuition for the remaining academic year, they did provide spending money for me.

5. Challenges Sharpen Your Grit

Challenges make you more determined to reach your goal. It's not a rarity that highly successful people credit their resilience and persistence (aka "grit") as one of the main reasons for their success. Rather than seeing defeats and disappointment as hindrances to their growth, they wholeheartedly believe that their past failures were the fuel they needed to propel them to greatness. People who have never been challenged in life do not have the opportunity to learn how to overcome adversity, a crucial element in developing coping strategies, character, and strength. As a result, they find themselves giving up far too easily when the going gets tough, compared to those who have learned to embrace challenges and use them to their advantage.

My encouragement to you is to not give up on your dream because God will help you meet your challenges. Hang in there. Stay strong. Choose to have faith and believe the light at the end of the tunnel is just around corner.

I am reminded of the Biblical book of Ruth. This book challenges our easy assumptions and stereotypes regarding those who seek refuge in another country as immigrants, especially when we reduce them into two simple questions: "What challenges does Ruth face as she accompanies her mother-in-law to Judah?" and "How does God help her meet these challenges?" In the story of Ruth, which took place when there was no king in Israel and everyone did what was right in their own eyes (Judge 17:6), Ruth moved from being a Moabite foreigner to a valued community member. Ruth's amazing transformation of status was due to the discerning eye and generous heart of Boaz, to whom she marveled: "Why have I found favor in your sight, that you should take notice of me when I am a foreigner?" (Ruth 2:10). Boaz fed and protected Ruth as she gleaned grain from his fields. The people of Israel carefully distinguished among the other persons who lived among them. They used "zar" and "nokri" ("foreigner") to describe those like the Canaanites, Ammonites, and Moabites who had no part in Israel, but used "ger" ("alien" or "sojourner") for one "who comes from outside the community but who settles within the community," Dana Wilbanks has noted. "The ger is very much like what we today call a "resident alien." He or she may be a refugee or an immigrant, settling into the community but still being an outsider who brings a different communal identity. Within the covenant community, however, this difference does not justify a double standard of justice."[17]

So, like Ruth, you will be cared for and supported by the "Boazes" living in our country, regardless of the issues surrounding immigration, and you will fulfill your dream. May this book inspire you never to give up on your dreams and to keep going toward the life that you've always imagined!

Final Thoughts

There you have it, five great silver linings that can be found even in your darkest times. Remember that when the going gets tough, life is presenting you with a big opportunity for growth and progress. So, grab it and never look back. It may be far from easy, but if you use them wisely, challenges can serve as catalysts pushing you to become the best version of yourself!

Let me offer a prayer for you:

God of creation, I know that your redeeming work in this world is not dictated by borders, by lines on a map. We praise You for the unreserved nature of Your mercy and the expansive reach of Your love. You have created all the people of the earth in Your image, including the one who is reading this book, and you do care for each one of us. Remind us this day of your call for us to be a blessing to all families of the earth and illuminate the fear that makes us unwilling to be the vessels of your blessing to those who live as strangers among us. Lord, I also pray for strength and pcrscvcrancc for the readers of my story to endure the trials and challenges of life. Help them to remain steadfast, trusting in Your promises and Your goodness. Give them strength to keep moving forward, even when it seems impossible, knowing that with You, all things are possible. I pray in Jesus' name. Amen.

About the Author

Eddie Tokpa is the founder of Msingi Soccer Academy, a nonprofit organization based in Uganda that uses the game of soccer as a platform to provide vulnerable and disadvantaged young people with educational opportunities, life skills development, and mentorship. He's also the co-founder of Msingi Development Fund, a 501(c)3 based in the US that supports the work of Msingi Soccer Academy. Before his current job, he was an assistant coordinator for the Uganda Studies Program, a study abroad organization at the Uganda Christian University (UCU) in Uganda.

Born and raised in Liberia, Eddie lives in Colorado with his wife, Lisa, and their son, Zeke. He continues his fight against cancer and seeks to provide support to others facing challenging circumstances. He prays that his life story will be an inspiration to others and that his story will inspire them to look for God's fingerprints on their current situation and circumstances.

Notes

1 Christopher Clapham, *Liberia, and Sierra Leone: An Essay in Comparative Politics* Cambridge: Cambridge University Press, 1976, p.53.
2 ibid, statistical appendix, p.130
3 https://www.theperspective.org/2010/0327201001.html
4 Prof. Justin B. Mudekereza *Understanding the Multifaceted Management Problems of Refugee Resettlement in the United States of America* (2018) Dorrance Publishing company P.1.
5 Jack C. Miller, "The Homeless of Africa,"*Africa Today* 29 (1982.P.5.)
6 Michel Agier *On the Margin of the World: The Refugee Experience Today* (2005) Cambridge: Polity Press, P.28
7 Mats Utas "Assiduous Exile: Strategies of Work and Integration Among Liberian Refugees in Danane, Ivory Coast" *Liberian Studies Journal* (2004) 29:33-58.
8 Stephanie Owen and Isabelle Sawhill "Should Everyone Go to College?" *Brooking Report* (2010)
9 McAndrew, F. T. "The measurement of 'rootedness' and the prediction of attachment to hometowns in college students" Journal of Environmental Psychology, 18, (1998) 409-417.
10 Mary Yuan *Where is Home? A Travel Memoir of Belonging, Healing, and Identity.* New Degree Press (2020)
11 Fretz, R.I. & Shaw L.L. *Writing Ethnographic Fieldnotes* (2011)

12 Baumeister, R.F. and Leary, M.R. *The Need to Belong: Desire for Interpersonal Attachments as Human Motivations* Psycho Bull (1995) 117:497-529

13 Peter Garrett, *Attitudes to Language,* Cambridge University Press, New York (2010)

14 Thurber CA, Walton EA. *Homesickness and Adjustment in University Students,* Journal of American College Health (2012) 60:415-419.

15 Severe Covid-19 GWAS Group. Ellinghaus D., Degenhardt F., Bujanda L., et al. *Genomewide association study of severe Covid-19 with respiratory failure.* N Engl J Med. 2020;383(16):1522–1534. doi: 10.1056/NEJMoa2020283. [PMC free article] [PubMed] [CrossRef] [Google Scholar]

16 Mhatma Gandhi, *Gandhi An Autobiography: The Story Of my Experiment with Truth* Beacon Press Books,1993

17 Dana W. Wilbanks, *Re-creating America: The Ethics of US Immigration and Refugee Policy in a Christian Perspective* Abingdon Press, Nashville, TN (1996, 99)

Printed in the USA
CPSIA information can be obtained
at www.ICGtesting.com
CBHW021605190424
7209CB00042B/934